OLD PORTRAITS

AND

MODERN SKETCHES.

—BY—

JOHN G. WHITTIER.

NEW YORK:

HURST & COMPANY.

PUBLISHERS.

ARGYLE PRESS,
PRINTING AND BOOKBINDING,
265 & 267 CHERRY ST., N. Y.

TO DR. G. BAILEY,

OF THE NATIONAL ERA,

Washington, D. C.

These Sketches, many of which originally appeared in the columns of the paper under his editorial supervision, are, in their present form, offered as a token of the esteem and confidence which years of political and literary communion have justified and confirmed, on the part of his friend and associate,

THE AUTHOR.

CONTENTS.

OLD PORTRAITS

AND

MODERN SKETCHES.

JOHN BUNYAN.

> Wouldst see
> A man i' the clouds, and hear him speak to thee?

WHO has not read Pilgrim's Progress? Who has not, in childhood, followed the wandering Christian on his way to the Celestial City? Who has not laid at night his young head on the pillow, to paint on the walls of darkness pictures of the Wicket Gate and the Archers, the Hill of Difficulty, the Lions and Giants, Doubting Castle and Vanity Fair, the sunny Delectable Mountains and the Shepherds, the Black River and the wonderful glory beyond it; and at last fallen asleep, to dream over the strange story, to hear the sweet welcomings of the sisters at the House Beautiful, and the song of birds from the window of that "upper chamber which opened toward the sunrising?" And who, looking back to the green spots in his childish experiences, does not bless the good Tinker of Elstow?

And who, that has reperused the Story of the Pilgrim at a maturer age, and felt the plummet of its truth sounding in the deep places of the soul, has not reason to bless the author for some timely warning or grateful encouragement? Where is the scholar, the poet, the man of taste and feeling, who does not, with Cowper,

> Even in transitory life's late day,
> Revere the man whose Pilgrim marks the road
> And guides the Progress of the soul to God!

We have just been reading, with no slight degree of interest, that simple but wonderful piece of autobiography, entitled "Grace Abounding to the Chief of Sinners," from the pen of the author of Pilgrim's Progress. It is the record of a journey more terrible than that of the ideal Pilgrim; "truth stranger than fiction"; the painful upward struggling of a spirit from the blackness of despair and blasphemy, into the high, pure air of Hope and Faith. More earnest words were never written. It is the entire unveiling of a human heart; the tearing off of the fig-leaf covering of its sin. The voice which speaks to us from these old pages seems not so much that of a denizen of the world in which we live, as of a soul at the last solemn confessional. Shorn of all ornament, simple and direct as the contrition and prayer of childhood, when for the first time the Specter of Sin stands by its bedside, the style is that of a man dead to self-gratification, careless of the world's opinion, and only desirous to convey to others, in all truthfulness and sincerity, the lesson of his inward trials, temptations, sins, weaknesses, and dangers; and to give glory to Him who had mercifully led him through all, and enabled him, like his own Pilgrim, to leave behind the Valley of the Shadow of Death, the snares of the Enchanted Ground, and the terrors of Doubting Castle, and to reach the land of Beulah, where the air was sweet and pleasant, and the birds sang and the flowers sprang up around him, and the Shining Ones walked in the brightness of the not distant Heaven. In the introductory pages he says: "I could have dipped into a style higher than this in which I have discoursed, and could have adorned all things more than here I have seemed to do; but I dared not. God did not play in tempting me; neither did I play when I sunk, as it were, into a bottomless pit, when the pangs of hell took hold on me; wherefore, I may not play in relating of them, but be plain and simple, and lay down the thing as it was."

This book, as well as Pilgrim's Progress, was written in Bedford Prison, and was designed especially for the comfort and edification of his "children, whom God had counted him worthy to beget in faith by his ministry." In his introduction he tells them, that, although taken from them, and tied up, "sticking, as it were, between the teeth of the lions of the wilderness," he once again, as before, from the top of Shemer and Hermon, so now, from the lion's den and the mountain of leopards, would look after them with fatherly care and desires for their everlasting welfare. "If," said he, "you have sinned against light; if you are tempted to blaspheme; if you are drowned in despair; if you think God fights against you; or if Heaven is hidden from your eyes, remember it was so with your father. But out of all the Lord delivered me."

He gives no dates; he affords scarcely a clew to his localities; of the man, as he worked, and ate, and drank, and lodged; of his neighbors and contemporaries; of all he saw and heard of the world about him, we have only an occasional glimpse, here and there, in his narrative. It is the story of his inward life only that he relates. What had time and place to do with one who trembled always with the awful consciousness of an immortal nature, and about whom fell alternately the shadows of hell and the splendors of heaven? We gather, indeed, from his record, that he was not an idle on-looker in the time of England's great struggle for freedom, but a soldier of the Parliament, in his young years, among the praying sworders and psalm-singing pikemen, the Greathearts and Holdfasts whom he has immortalized in his allegory; but the only allusion which he makes to this portion of his experience is by way of illustration of the goodness of God in preserving him on occasions of peril.

He was born at Elstow, in Bedfordshire, in 1628; and, to use his own words, "his father's house was of that rank which is the meanest and most despised of all the families of the land." His father was a tinker, and the son followed the same calling, which necessarily brought him into association with the lowest and most depraved classes of English society. The estimation in which the tinker and his occupation were held, in the seventeenth century, may be learned from the quaint and humorous description of Sir Thomas Overbury. "The tinker," saith he, "is a movable, for he hath no abiding in one place; he seems to be devout, for his life is a continual pilgrimage, and sometimes, in humility, goes barefoot, therein making necessity a virtue; he is a gallant, for he carries all his wealth upon his back; or a philosopher, for he bears all his substance with him. He is always furnished with a song, to which his hammer, keeping tune, proves that he was the first founder of the kettle-drum; where the best ale is, there stands his music most upon crotchets. The companion of his travel is some foul, sunburnt quean, that, since the terrible statute, has recanted gipsyism, and is turned pedleress. So marches he all over England, with his bag and baggage; his conversation is irreprovable, for he is always mending. He observes truly the statutes, and therefore had rather steal than beg. He is so strong an enemy of idleness, that in mending one hole he would rather make three than want work; and when he hath done, he throws the wallet of his faults behind him. His tongue is very voluble, which, with canting, proves him a linguist. He is entertained in every place, yet enters no farther than the door, to avoid suspicion. To conclude, if he escape Tyburn and Banbury, he dies a beggar."

Truly, but a poor beginning for a pious life was the youth of John Bunyan. As might have been expected, he was a wild, reckless, swearing boy, as his father doubtless was before him. "It was my delight," says he, "to be taken captive by the devil. I had few equals, both for cursing and swearing, lying and blaspheming." Yet, in his ignorance and darkness, his powerful imagination early lent terror to the reproaches of conscience. He was scared, even in childhood, with dreams of hell and apparitions of devils. Troubled with fears of eternal fire, and the malignant demons who fed it in the regions of despair, he says that he often wished either that there was no hell, or that he had been born a devil himself, that he might be a tormentor rather than one of the tormented.

At an early age he appears to have married. His wife was as poor as himself, for he tells us that they had not so much as a dish or spoon between them; but she brought with her two books on religious subjects, the reading of which seems to have had no slight degree of influence on his mind. He went to church regularly, adored the priest and all things pertaining to his office, being, as he says, "overrun with superstition." On one occasion, a sermon was preached against the breach of the Sabbath by sports or labor, which struck him at the moment as especially designed for himself; but by the time he had finished his dinner, he was prepared to "shake it out of his mind, and return to his sports and gaming."

"But the same day," he continues, "as I was in the midst of a game of cat, and having struck it one blow from the hole, just as I was about to strike it a second time, a voice did suddenly dart from Heaven into my soul, which said, 'Wilt thou leave thy sins and go to heaven, or have thy sins and go to hell?' At this, I was put to an exceeding maze; wherefore, leaving my cat upon the ground, I looked up to Heaven, and it was, as if I had, with the eyes of my understanding, seen the Lord Jesus look down upon me, as being very hotly displeased with me, and as if he did severely threaten me with some grievous punishment for those and other ungodly practices.

"I had no sooner thus conceived in my mind, but suddenly this conclusion fastened on my spirit (for the former hint did set my sins again before my face), that I had been a great and grievous sinner, and that it was now too late for me to look after Heaven; for Christ would not forgive me nor pardon my transgressions. Then, while I was thinking of it, and fearing lest it should be so, I felt my heart sink in despair, concluding it was too late; and therefore I resolved in my mind to go on in sin; for, thought I, if the case be thus, my state is surely miserable; miserable if I leave my sins, and but miserable if I follow them; I can but be damned; and if I must be so, I had as good be damned for many sins as be damned for few."

The reader of Pilgrim's Progress cannot fail here to call to mind the wicked suggestions of the Giant to Christian in the dungeon of Doubting Castle.

"I returned," he says, "desperately to my sport again; and I well remember, that presently this kind of despair did so possess my soul, that I was persuaded I could never attain to other comfort than what I should get in sin; for Heaven was gone already, so that on that I must not think; wherefore, I found within me great desire to take my fill of sin, that I might taste the sweetness of it; and I made as much haste as I could to fill my belly with its delicates, lest I should die before I had my desires; for that I feared greatly. In these things, I protest before God, I lie not, neither do I frame this sort of speech; these were really, strongly, and with all my heart, my desires; the good Lord, whose mercy is unsearchable, forgive my transgressions."

One day, while standing in the street, cursing and blaspheming, he met with a reproof which startled him. The woman of the house, in front of which the wicked young tinker was standing, herself, as he remarks, "a very loose, ungodly wretch," protested that his horrible profanity made her tremble; that he was the ungodliest fellow for swearing she had ever heard, and able to spoil all the youth of the town who came in his company. Struck by this wholly unexpected rebuke, he at once abandoned the practice of swearing; although previously he tells that "he had never known how to speak, unless he put an oath before and another behind."

The good name which he gained by this change was now a temptation to him. "My neighbors," he says, "were amazed at my great conversion from prodigious profaneness to something like a moral life and sober man. Now, therefore, they began to praise, to commend, and to speak well of me, both to my face and behind my back. Now I was, as they said, become godly; now I was become a right honest man. But oh! when I understood those were their words and opinions of me, it pleased me mighty well; for though as yet I was nothing but a poor painted hypocrite, yet I loved to be talked of as one that was truly godly. I was proud of my godliness, and, indeed, I did all I did either to be seen of or well spoken of by men; and thus I continued for about a twelvemonth or more."

The tyranny of his imagination at this period is seen in the following relation of his abandonment of one of his favorite sports.

"Now you must know, that before this I had taken much delight in ringing, but my conscience beginning to be tender, I thought such practice was but vain, and therefore forced myself to leave it; yet my mind hankered; wherefore, I would go to the steeple-house and look on, though I durst not ring; but I thought this did not become religion neither; yet I forced myself, and would look on still. But quickly after, I began to think, 'How if one of the bells should fall?' Then I chose to stand under a main beam, that lay overthwart the steeple, from side to side, thinking here I might stand sure; but then I thought again, should the bell fall with a swing, it might first hit the wall, and then, rebounding upon me, might kill me for all this beam. This made me stand in the steeple door; and now, thought I, I am safe enough; for if a bell should then fall, I can slip out behind these thick walls, and so be preserved notwithstanding.

"So after this I would yet go to see them ring, but would not go any farther than the steeple door. But then it came in my head, 'How if the steeple itself should fall?' And this thought (it may, for aught I know, when I stood and looked on) did continually so shake my mind, that I durst not stand at the steeple door any longer, but was forced to flee, for fear the steeple should fall upon my head."

About this time, while wandering through Bedford in pursuit of employment, he chanced to see three or four poor old women sitting at a door, in the evening sun, and, drawing near them, heard them converse upon the things of God; of His work in their hearts; of their natural depravity; of the temptations of the Adversary; and of the joy of believing, and of the peace of reconciliation. The words of the aged women found a response in the soul of the listener. "He felt his heart shake," to use his own words; he saw that he lacked the true tokens of a Christian. He now forsook the company of the profane and licentious, and sought that of a poor man who had the reputation of piety, but, to his grief, he found him "a devilish ranter, given up to all manner of uncleanness; he would laugh at all exhortations to sobriety, and deny that there was a God, an angel, or a spirit."

"Neither," he continues, "was this man only a temptation to me, but, my calling lying in the country, I happened to come into several people's company, who, though strict in religion formerly, yet were also drawn away by these ranters. These would also talk with me of their ways, and condemn me as illegal and dark; pretending that they only had attained to perfection, that could do what they would, and not sin. Oh! these temptations were suitable to my flesh, I being but a young man, and my nature in its prime; but God, who had, as I hope, designed me for better things, kept me in the fear of his name, and did not suffer me to accept such cursed principles."

At this time he was sadly troubled to ascertain whether or not he had that faith which the Scriptures spake of. Traveling one day from Elstow to Bedford, after a recent rain, which had left pools of water in the path, he felt a strong desire to settle the question by commanding the pools to become dry, and the dry places to become pools. Going under the hedge to pray for ability to work the miracle, he was struck with the thought, that if he failed he should know, indeed, that he was a castaway, and give himself up to despair. He dared not attempt the experiment, and went on his way, to use his own forcible language, "tossed up and down between the devil and his own ignorance."

Soon after, he had one of those visions which foreshadowed the wonderful dream of his Pilgrim's Progress. He saw some holy people of Bedford on the sunny side of an high mountain, refreshing themselves in the pleasant air and sunlight, while he was shivering in cold and darkness, amidst snows and never-melting ices, like the victims of the Scandinavian hell. A wall compassed the mountain, separating him from the blessed, with one small gap or doorway, through which, with great pain and effort, he was at last enabled to work his way into the sunshine, and sit down with the saints, in the light and warmth thereof.

But now a new trouble assailed him. Like Milton's metaphysical spirits, who sat apart,

> And reasoned of foreknowledge, will, and fate,

he grappled with one of those great questions which have always perplexed and baffled human inquiry, and upon which much has been written to little purpose. He was tortured with anxiety to know whether, according to the Westminster formula, he was elected to salvation or damnation. His old adversary vexed his soul with evil suggestions, and even quoted Scripture to enforce them. "It may be you are not elected," said the Tempter, and the poor tinker thought the supposition altogether too probable. "Why, then," said Satan, "you had as good leave off, and strive no farther; for if, indeed, you should not be elected and chosen of God, there is no hope of your being saved; for it is neither in him that willeth nor in him that runneth, but in

God who showeth mercy." At length when, as he says, he was about giving up the ghost of all his hopes, this passage fell with weight upon his spirit; "Look at the generations of old, and see; did ever any trust in God, and were confounded?" Comforted by these words, he opened his Bible to note them, but the most diligent search and inquiry of his neighbors failed to discover them. At length, his eye fell upon them in the Apocryphal book of Ecclesiasticus. This, he says, somewhat doubted him at first, as the book was not canonical; but in the end he took courage and comfort from the passage. "I bless God," he says, "for that word; it was good for me. That word doth still oftentimes shine before my face."

A long and weary struggle was now before him. "I cannot," he says, "express with what longings and breathings of my soul I cried unto Christ to call me. Gold! could it have been gotten by gold, what would I have given for it. Had I a whole world, it had all gone ten thousand times over for this, that my soul might have been in a converted state. How lovely now was every one in my eyes, that I thought to be converted men and women. They shone, they walked like a people who carried the broad seal of Heaven with them."

With what force and intensity of language does he portray, in the following passage, the reality and earnestness of his agonizing experience:

"While I was thus afflicted with the fears of my own damnation, there were two things would make me wonder: the one was, when I saw old people hunting after the things of this life, as if they should live here always; the other was, when I found professors much distressed and cast down, when they met with outward losses; as of husband, wife, or child. Lord, thought I, what a seeking after carnal things by some, and what grief in others for the loss of them! If they so much labor after and shed so many tears for the things of this present life, how am I to be bemoaned, pitied, and prayed for! My soul is dying, my soul is damning. Were my soul but in a good condition, and were I but sure of it, ah! how rich should I esteem myself, though blessed but with bread and water! I should count these but small afflictions, and should bear them as little burdens. 'A wounded spirit who can bear!'"

He looked with envy, as he wandered through the country, upon the birds in the trees, the hares in the preserves, and the fishes in the streams. They were happy in their brief existence, and their death was but a sleep. He felt himself alienated from God, a discord in the harmonies of the universe. The very rooks which fluttered around the old church spire seemed more worthy of the Creator's love and care than himself. A vision of the infernal fire, like that glimpse of hell which was afforded to Christian by the Shepherds, was continually before him, with its "rumbling noise, and the cry of some tormented, and the scent of brimstone." Whithersoever he went, the glare of it scorched him, and its dreadful sound was in his ears. His vivid but disturbed imagination lent new terrors to the awful figures by which the sacred writers conveyed the idea of future retribution to the Oriental mind. Bunyan's World of Woe, if it lacked the colossal architecture and solemn vastness of Milton's Pandemonium, was more clearly defined; its agonies were within the pale of human comprehension; its victims were men and women, with the same keen sense of corporeal suffering which they possessed in life; and who, to use his own terrible description, had "all the loathed variety of hell to grapple with; fire unquenchable, a lake of choking brimstone, eternal chains, darkness more black than night, the everlasting gnawing of the worm, the sight of devils, and the yells and outcries of the damned."

His mind at this period was evidently shaken in some degree from its balance. He was troubled with strange wicked thoughts, confused by doubts and blasphemous suggestions, for which he could only account by supposing himself possessed of the devil. He wanted to curse and swear, and had to clap his hands on his mouth to prevent it. In prayer, he felt, as he supposed, Satan behind him, pulling his clothes, and telling him to have done, and break off; suggesting that he had better pray to him, and calling up before his mind's eye the figures of a bull, a tree, or some other object, instead of the awful idea of God.

He notes here, as cause of thankfulness, that, even in this dark and clouded state, he was enabled to see the "vile and abominable things fomented by the

Quakers," to be errors. Gradually, the shadow wherein he had so long

> Walked beneath the day's broad glare,
> A darkened man,

passed from him, and for a season he was afforded an "evidence of his salvation from Heaven, with many golden seals thereon hanging in his sight." But, ere long, other temptations assailed him. A strange suggestion haunted him, to sell or part with his Saviour. His own account of this hallucination is too painfully vivid to awaken any other feeling than that of sympathy and sadness.

"I could neither eat my food, stoop for a pin, chop a stick, or cast mine eye to look on this or that, but still the temptation would come, Sell Christ for this, or sell Christ for that; sell him, sell him.

"Sometimes it would run in my thoughts, not so little as a hundred times together, Sell him, sell him; against which, I may say, for whole hours together, I have been forced to stand as continually leaning and forcing my spirit against it, lest haply, before I were aware, some wicked thought might arise in my heart, that might consent thereto; and sometimes the tempter would make me believe I had consented to it; but then I should be as tortured upon a rack, for whole days together.

"This temptation did put me to such scares, lest I should at sometimes, I say, consent thereto, and be overcome therewith, that, by the very force of my mind, my very body would be put into action or motion, by way of pushing or thrusting with my hands or elbows; still answering—as fast as the destroyer said, Sell him,—I will not, I will not, I will not; no, not for thousands, thousands, thousands of worlds; thus reckoning, lest I should set too low a value on him, even until I scarce well knew where I was, or how to be composed again.

"But to be brief: one morning, as I did lie in my bed, I was, as at other times, most fiercely assaulted with this temptation, to sell and part with Christ; the wicked suggestion still running in my mind, Sell him, sell him, sell him, sell him, sell him, as fast as a man could speak; against which, also, in my mind, as at other times, I answered, No, no, not for thousands, thousands, thousands—at least twenty times together; but at last, after much striving, I felt this thought pass through my heart, *Let him go if he will;* and I thought also, that I felt my heart freely consent thereto. Oh! the diligence of Satan! Oh! the desperateness of man's heart!

"Now was the battle won, and down fell I, as a bird that is shot from the top of a tree, into great guilt, and fearful despair. Thus getting out of my bed, I went moping into the field; but God knows, with as heavy a heart as mortal man, I think, could bear; where, for the space of two hours, I was like a man bereft of life; and, as now, past all recovery, and bound over to eternal punishment.

"And withal, that Scripture did seize upon my soul: 'Or profane person, as Esau, who, for one morsel of meat, sold his birthright; for ye know how that afterward, when he would have inherited the blessing, he was rejected; for he found no place for repentance, though he sought it carefully with tears.'"

For two years and a half, as he informs us, that awful Scripture sounded in his ears like the knell of a lost soul. He believed that he had committed the unpardonable sin. His mental anguish was united with bodily illness and suffering. His nervous system became fearfully deranged; his limbs trembled, and he supposed this visible tremulousness and agitation to be the mark of Cain. Troubled with pain and distressing sensations in his chest, he began to fear that his breast-bone would split open, and that he should perish like Judas Iscariot. He feared the tiles of the houses would fall upon him as he walked the streets. He was like his own Man in the Cage at the House of the Interpreter, shut out from the promises, and looking forward to certain judgment. "Methought," he says, "the very sun that shineth in heaven did grudge to give me light." And still the dreadful words, "He found no place for repentance, though he sought it carefully with tears," sounded in the depths of his soul. They were, he says, like fetters of brass to his legs, and their continual clanking followed him for months. Regarding himself elected and predestined for damnation, he thought that all things worked for his damage and eternal overthrow, while all things wrought for the best, and to do good to the elect and called of God unto salvation. God and all His universe had, he thought, conspired against him; the green earth, the bright waters, the sky itself, were written over with his irrevocable curse.

Well was it said by Bunyan's contemporary, the excellent Cudworth, in his eloquent sermon before the Long Parliament, that "we are nowhere commanded to pry into the secrets of God, but the wholesome advice given us is this: 'To *make* our calling and election sure.' We have no warrant from Scripture to peep into the hidden rolls of eternity, to spell out our names among the stars." "Must we say that God sometimes, to exercise His uncontrollable dominion, delights rather in plunging wretched souls down into infernal night and everlasting darkness? What, then, shall we make the God of the whole world? Nothing but a cruel and dreadful *Errinys*, with curled fiery snakes about His head, and firebrands in His hand; thus governing the world! Surely this will make us either secretly think there is no God in the world, if He must needs be such, or else to wish heartily there were none." It was thus at times with Bunyan. He was tempted, in this season of despair, to believe that there was no resurrection and no judgment.

One day, he tells us, a sudden rushing sound, as of wind or the wings of angels, came to him through the window, wonderfully sweet and pleasant; and it was as if a voice spoke to him from heaven words of encouragement and hope, which, to use his language, commanded, for the time, "a silence in his heart to all those tumultuous thoughts that did use, like masterless hell-hounds, to roar and bellow and make a hideous noise within him." About this time, also, some comforting passages of Scripture were called to mind; but he remarks, that whenever he strove to apply them to his case, Satan would thrust the curse of Esau in his face, and wrest the good word from him. The blessed promise, "Him that cometh to me, I will in no wise cast out," was the chief instrumentality in restoring his lost peace. He says of it: "If ever Satan and I did strive for any word of God in all my life, it was for this good word of Christ; he at one end, and I at the other; oh, what work we made! It was for this in John, I say, that we did so tug and strive; he pulled, and I pulled, but, God be praised! I overcame him; I got sweetness from it. Oh! many a pull hath my heart had with Satan for this blessed sixth chapter of John!"

Who does not here call to mind the struggle between Christian and Apollyon in the valley! That was no fancy sketch; it was the narrative of the author's own grapple with the Spirit of Evil. Like his ideal Christian, he "conquered through Him that loved him." Love wrought the victory: the Scripture of Forgiveness overcame that of Hatred.

He never afterward relapsed into that state of religious melancholy from which he so hardly escaped. He speaks of his deliverance, as the waking out of a troublesome dream. His painful experience was not lost upon him; for it gave him, ever after, a tender sympathy for the weak, the sinful, the ignorant, and desponding. In some measure, he had been "touched with the feeling of their infirmities." He could feel for those in the bonds of sin and despair, as bound with them. Hence his power as a preacher; hence the wonderful adaptation of his great allegory to all the variety of spiritual conditions. Like Fearing, he had lain a month in the Slough of Despond, and had played, like him, the long, melancholy bass of spiritual heaviness. With Feeble-mind, he had fallen into the hands of Slay-good, of the nature of Man-eaters; and had limped along his difficult way upon the crutches of Ready-to-halt. Who better than himself could describe the condition of Despondency, and his daughter Much-afraid, in the dungeon of Doubting Castle? Had he not also fallen among thieves, like Little-faith?

His account of his entering upon the solemn duties of a preacher of the gospel is at once curious and instructive. He deals honestly with himself, exposing all his various moods, weaknesses, doubts and temptations. "I preached," he says, "what I felt; for the terrors of the law and the guilt of transgression lay heavy on my conscience. I have been as one sent to them from the dead. I went myself in chains to preach to them in chains; and carried that fire in my conscience which I persuaded them to beware of." At times, when he stood up to preach, blasphemies and evil doubts rushed into his mind, and he felt a strong desire to utter them aloud to his congregation; and at other seasons, when he was about to apply to the sinner some searching and fearful text of Scripture, he was tempted to withhold it, on the ground that it condemned himself also; but, withstanding the suggestion of the Tempter, to use his own simile, he bowed himself like Samson to condemn sin wherever he found it, though he brought guilt and condemnation upon himself thereby, choosing rather to die with the Philistines, than to deny the truth.

Foreseeing the consequences of exposing himself to the operation of the penal laws, by holding conventicles and preaching, he was deeply afflicted at the thought of the suffering and destitution to which his wife and children might be exposed by his death or imprisonment. Nothing can be more touching than his simple and earnest words on this point. They show how warm and deep were his human affections, and what a tender and loving heart he laid as a sacrifice on the altar of duty:

"I found myself a man compassed with infirmities; the parting with my wife and poor children hath often been to me, in this place, as the pulling the flesh from the bones; and also it brought to my mind the many hardships, miseries, and wants that my poor family was like to meet with, should I be taken from them, especially my poor blind child, who lay nearer my heart than all beside. Oh! the thoughts of the hardships I thought my poor blind one might go under, would break my heart to pieces.

"Poor child! thought I, what sorrow art thou like

to have for thy portion in this world! thou must be beaten, must beg, suffer hunger, cold, nakedness, and a thousand calamities, though I cannot now endure the wind should blow upon thee. But yet, thought I, I must venture you all with God, though it goeth to the quick to leave you. Oh! I saw I was as a man who was pulling down his house upon the heads of his wife and children; yet I thought on those 'two milch kine that were to carry the ark of God into another country, and to leave their calves behind them.'

"But that which helped me in this temptation was divers considerations: the first was, the consideration of those two Scriptures, 'Leave thy fatherless children, I will preserve them alive; and let thy widows trust in me'; and again, 'The Lord said, verily it shall go well with thy remnant; verily I will cause the enemy to entreat them well in the time of evil.'"

He was arrested in 1660, charged with ' devilishly and perniciously abstaining from church," and of being "a common upholder of conventicles." At the quarter sessions, where his trial seems to have been conducted somewhat like that of Faithful at Vanity Fair, he was sentenced to perpetual banishment. This sentence, however, was never executed, but he was remanded to Bedford jail, where he lay a prisoner for twelve years.

Here, shut out from the world, with no other books than the Bible and Fox's Martyrs, he penned that great work which has attained a wider and more stable popularity than any other book in the English tongue. It is alike the favorite of the nursery and the study. Many experienced Christians hold it only second to the Bible; the infidel himself would not willingly let it die. Men of all sects read it with delight, as in the main a truthful representation of the Christian pilgrimage; without, indeed, assenting to all the doctrines which the author puts in the mouth of his fighting sermonizer, Greatheart, or which may be deduced from some other portions of his allegory. A recollection of his fearful sufferings, from misapprehension of a single text in the Scriptures, relative to the question of election, we may suppose gave a milder tone to the theology of his Pilgrim than was altogether consistent with the Calvinism of the seventeenth century. "Religion," says Macaulay, "has scarcely ever worn a form so calm and soothing as in Bunyan's allegory." In composing it, he seems never to have altogether lost sight of the fact, that, in his life and death struggle with Satan for the blessed promise recorded by the Apostle of Love, the adversary was generally found on the Genevan side of the argument.

Little did the short-sighted persecutors of Bunyan dream, when they closed upon him the door of Bedford jail, that God would overrule their poor spite and envy to his own glory and the world-wide renown of their victim. In the solitude of his prison, the ideal forms of beauty and sublimity, which had long flitted before him vaguely, like the vision of the Temanite, took shape and coloring; and he was endowed with power to reduce them to order and arrange them in harmonious groupings. His powerful imagination, no longer self-tormenting, but under the direction of reason and grace, expanded his narrow cell into a vast theater, lighted up for the display of its wonders. To this creative faculty of his mind might have been aptly applied the language which George Wither, a contemporary prisoner, addressed to his Muse:

> The dull loneness, the black shade
> Which these hanging vaults have made,
> The rude portals that give light
> More to terror than delight;
> This my chamber of neglect,
> Walled about with disrespect,—
> From all these, and this dull air,
> A fit object for despair,
> She hath taught me by her might,
> To draw comfort and delight.

That stony cell of his was to him like the rock of Padan-aram to the wandering Patriarch. He saw angels ascending and descending. The House Beautiful rose up before him, and its holy sisterhood welcomed him. He looked, with his Pilgrim, from the Chamber of Peace. The Valley of Humiliation lay stretched out beneath his eye, and he heard "the curious melodious note of the country birds, who sing all the day long in the spring time, when the flowers appear, and the sun shines warm, and make the woods and groves and solitary places glad." Side by side with the good Christiana and the loving Mercy, he walked through the green and lowly valley, "fruitful as any the crow flies over," through "meadows beautiful with lilies"; the song of the poor but fresh-faced shepherd boy, who lived a merry life, and wore the herb *heartsease* in his bosom, sounded through his cell:

> He that is down need fear no fall;
> He that is low no pride.

The broad and pleasant "river of the Water of Life" glided peacefully before him, fringed "on either side with green trees, with all manner of fruit," and leaves of healing, with "meadows beautified with lilies, and green all the year long"; he saw the Delectable Mountains, glorious with sunshine, overhung with gardens and orchards and vineyards; and beyond all, the Land of Beulah, with its eternal sunshine, its song of birds, its music of fountains, its purple, clustered vines, and groves through which walked the Shining Ones, silver-winged and beautiful.

What were bars and bolts and prison walls to him, whose eyes were anointed to see, and whose ears opened to hear, the glory and the rejoicing of the City of God, when the pilgrims were conducted to its golden gates, from the black and bitter river, with the sounding trumpeters, the transfigured harpers with their crowns of gold, the sweet voices of angels, the welcoming peal of bells in the holy city, and the songs of the redeemed ones? In reading the concluding pages of the first part of Pilgrim's Progress, we feel as if the mysterious glory of the Beatific Vision was unveiled before us. We are dazzled with the excess of light. We are entranced with the mighty melody; overwhelmed by the great anthem of rejoicing spirits. It can only be adequately described in the language of Milton in respect to the Apocalypse, as "a seven-fold chorus of hallelujahs and harping symphonies."

Few who read Bunyan now-a-days think of him as one of the brave old English confessors, whose steady and firm endurance of persecution baffled, and in the end overcame, the tyranny of the established church in the reign of Charles II. What Milton and Penn and Locke wrote in defense of Liberty, Bunyan lived out and acted. He made no concessions to worldly rank. Dissolute lords and proud bishops he counted less than the humblest and poorest of his disciples at Bedford. When first arrested and thrown into prison, he supposed he should be called to suffer death for his faithful testimony to the truth; and his great fear was, that he should not meet his fate with the requisite firmness, and so dishonor the cause of his Master. And when dark clouds came over him, and he sought in vain for a sufficient evidence that in the event of his death it would be well with him, he girded up his soul with the reflection that as he suffered for the word and way of God, he was engaged not to shrink one hair's breadth from it. "I will leap," he says, "off the ladder blindfold into eternity, sink or swim, come heaven, come hell

Lord Jesus, if thou wilt catch me, do; if not, I will venture in thy name!"

The English revolution of the seventeenth century, while it humbled the false and oppressive aristocracy of rank and title, was prodigal in the development of the real nobility of the mind and heart. Its history is bright with the footprints of men whose very names still stir the hearts of freemen, the world over, like a trumpet-peal. Say what we may of its fanaticism, laugh as we may at its extravagant enjoyment of newly acquired religious and civil liberty, who shall now venture to deny that it was the golden age of England? Who that regards freedom above slavery, will now sympathize with the outcry and lamentation of those interested in the continuance of the old order of things, against the prevalence of sects and schism, but who, at the same time, as Milton shrewdly intimates, dreaded more the rending of their pontifical sleeves than the rending of the church? Who shall now sneer at Puritanism, with the "Defense of Unlicensed Printing" before him? Who scoff at Quakerism over the Journal of George Fox? Who shall join with debauched lordlings and fat-witted prelates in ridicule of Anabaptist levelers and dippers, after rising from the perusal of Pilgrim's Progress? "There were giants in those days." And foremost amid that band of liberty-loving and God-fearing men,

> The slandered Calvinists of Charles's time,
> Who fought, and won it, Freedom's holy fight,

stands the subject of our sketch, the Tinker of Elstow. Of his high merit as an author there is no longer any question. The *Edinburgh Review* expressed the common sentiment of the literary world, when it declared that the two great creative minds of the seventeenth century were those which produced Paradise Lost and the Pilgrim's Progress.

THOMAS ELLWOOD.

COMMEND us to autobiographies! Give us the veritable notchings of Robinson Crusoe on his stick, the indubitable records of a life long since swallowed up in the blackness of darkness, traced by a hand the very dust of which has become undistinguishable. The foolish egotist who ever chronicled his daily experiences, his hopes and fears, poor plans and vain reachings after happiness, speaking to us out of the Past, and thereby giving us to understand that it was quite as real as our Present, is in no mean sort our benefactor, and commands our attention, in spite of his folly. We are thankful for the very vanity which prompted him to bottle up his poor records, and cast them into the great sea of Time, for future voyagers to pick up. We note, with the deepest interest, that in him too was enacted that miracle of a conscious existence, the reproduction of which in ourselves awes and perplexes us. He, too, had a mother; he hated and loved; the light from old-quenched hearts shone over him; he walked in the sunshine over the dust of those who had gone before him, just as we are now walking over his. These records of him remain, the footmarks of a long-extinct life; not of mere animal organism, but of a being like ourselves, enabling us, by studying their hieroglyphic significance, to decipher and see clearly into the mystery of existence centuries ago. The dead generations live again in these old self-biographies. Incidentally, unintentionally, yet in the simplest and most natural manner, they make us familiar with all the phenomena of life in the by-gone ages. We are brought in contact with actual flesh-and-blood men and women, not the ghostly outline figures which pass for such in what is called History. The horn lantern of the biographer, by the aid of which, with painful minuteness, he chronicled, from day to day, his own outgoings and incomings, making visible to us his pitiful wants, labors, trials, and tribulations, of the stomach and of the conscience, sheds, at times, a strong clear light upon contemporaneous activities; what seemed before half-fabulous, rises up in distinct and full proportions; we look at statesmen, philosophers, and poets with the eyes of those who lived perchance their next-door neighbors, and sold them beer, and mutton, and household stuffs, had access to their kitchens, and took note of the fashion of their wigs and the color of their breeches. Without some such light, all history would be just about as unintelligible and unreal as a dimly remembered dream.

The journals of the early Friends or Quakers are in this respect invaluable. Little, it is true, can be said, as a general thing, of their literary merits. Their authors were plain, earnest men and women, chiefly intent upon the substance of things, and having withal a strong testimony to bear against carnal wit and outside show and ornament. Yet, even the scholar may well admire the power of certain portions of George Fox's Journal, where a strong spirit clothes its utterance in simple, downright Saxon words; the quiet and beautiful enthusiasm of Pennington; the torrent energy of Edward Burrough; the serene wisdom of Penn; the logical acuteness of Barclay; the honest truthfulness of Sewell; the wit and humor of John Roberts (for even Quakerism had its apostolic jokers and drab-coated Robert Halls); and last, not least, the simple beauty of Woolman's Journal, the modest record of a life of good works and love.

Let us look at the "Life of Thomas Ellwood," The book before us is a hardly used Philadelphia reprint, bearing date of 1775. The original was published some sixty years before. It is not a book to be found in fashionable libraries, or noticed in fashionable reviews, but it is none the less deserving of attention.

Ellwood was born in 1639, in the little town of Crowell, in Oxfordshire. Old Walter, his father, was of "gentlemanly lineage," and held a commission of the peace under Charles I. One of his most intimate friends was Isaac Pennington, a gentleman of estate and good reputation, whose wife, the widow of Sir John Springette, was a lady of superior endowments. Her only daughter, Gulielma, was the playmate and companion of Thomas. On making this family a visit, in 1658, in company with his father, he was surprised to find that they had united with the Quakers, a sect then little known, and everywhere spoken against. Passing through the vista of nearly two centuries, let us cross the threshold, and look with the eyes of young Ellwood upon this Quaker family. It will doubtless give us a good idea of the earnest and solemn spirit of that age of religious awakening.

"So great a change from a free, debonair, and courtly sort of behavior, which we had formerly found there, into so strict a gravity as they now received us with, did not a little amuse us, and disappointed our expectations of such a pleasant visit as we had promised ourselves.

"For my part, I sought, and at length found means to cast myself into the company of the daughter, whom I found gathering flowers in the garden, attended by her maid, also a Quaker. But when I addressed her after my accustomed manner, with intention to engage her in discourse, on the foot of our former acquaintance, though she treated me with a courteous mien, yet, as young as she was, the gravity of her looks and behavior struck such an awe upon me that I found myself not so much master of myself as to pursue any further converse with her.

"We stayed dinner, which was very handsome, and lacked nothing to recommend it to me but the want of mirth and pleasant discourse, which we could neither have with them, nor, by reason of them, with one another; the weightiness which was upon their spirits and countenances keeping down the lightness that would have been up in ours."

Not long after, they made a second visit to their sober friends, spending several days, during which they attended a meeting in a neighboring farm-house, where we were introduced by Ellwood to two remarkable personages, Edward Burrough, the friend and fearless reprover of Cromwell, and by far the most eloquent preacher of his sect; and James Nayler, whose melancholy after-history of fanaticism, cruel sufferings, and beautiful repentance, is so well known to the readers of English history under the Protectorate. Under the preaching of these men, and the influence of the Pennington family, young Ellwood was brought into fellowship with the Quakers. Of the old Justice's sorrow and indignation at this sudden blasting of his hopes and wishes in respect to his son, and of the trials and difficulties of the latter in his new vocation, it is now scarcely worth while to speak. Let us step forward a few years, to 1662, considering meantime how matters, political and spiritual, are changed in that brief period. Cromwell, the Maccabeus of Puritanism, is no longer among men; Charles the Second sits in his place; profane and licentious cavaliers have thrust aside the sleek-haired, painful-faced Independents, who used to groan approval to the scriptural illustrations of Harrison and Fleetwood; men easy of virtue, without sincerity, either in religion or politics, occupying the places made honorable by the Miltons, Whitlocks, and Vanes of the Commonwealth. Having this change in view, the light which the farthing candle of Ellwood sheds upon one of these illustrious names will not be unwelcome. In his intercourse with Penn, and other learned Quakers, he had reason to lament his own deficiencies in scholarship, and his friend Pennington undertook to put him in a way of remedying the defect.

"He had," says Ellwood, "an intimate acquaintance with Dr. Paget, a physician of note in London, and he with John Milton, a gentleman of great note for learning throughout the learned world, for the accurate pieces he had written on various subjects and occasions.

"This person, having filled a public station in the former times, lived a private and retired life in London, and, having lost his sight, kept always a man to read for him, which usually was the son of some gentleman of his acquaintance, whom, in kindness, he took to improve in his learning.

"Thus, by the mediation of my friend Isaac Pennington with Dr. Paget, and through him with John Milton, was I admitted to come to him, not as a servant to him, nor to be in the house with him, but only to have the liberty of coming to his house at certain hours when I would, and read to him what books he should appoint, which was all the favor I desired.

"He received me courteously, as well for the sake of Dr. Paget, who introduced me, as of Isaac Pennington, who recommended me, to both of whom he bore a good respect. And, having inquired divers things of me, with respect to my former progression in learning, he dismissed me, to provide myself with such accommodations as might be most suitable to my studies.

"I went, therefore, and took lodgings as near to his house (which was then in Jewen Street) as I conveniently could, and from thenceforward went every day, in the afternoon, except on the first day of the week, and, sitting by him in his dining-room, read to him such books in the Latin tongue as he pleased to have me read.

"He perceiving with what earnest desire I had pursued learning, gave me not only all the encouragement, but all the help he could. For, having a curious ear, he understood by my tone when I understood what I read and when I did not, and accordingly would stop me, examine me, and open the most difficult passages to me."

Thanks, worthy Thomas, for this glimpse into John Milton's dining-room!

He had been with "Master Milton," as he calls him, only a few weeks, when, being one "first day morning," at the Bull and Mouth meeting, Aldersgate, the trainbands of the city, "with great noise and clamor," headed by Major Rosewell, fell upon him and his friends. The immediate cause of this onslaught upon quiet worshipers was the famous plot of the Fifth Monarchy men, grim old fanatics, who (like the Millerites of the present day) had been waiting long for the personal reign of Christ and the saints upon earth, and in their zeal to hasten such a consummation, had sallied into London streets with drawn swords and loaded matchlocks. The government took strong measures for suppressing dissenters' meetings or "conventicles"; and the poor Quakers, although not at all implicated in the disturbance, suffered more severely than any others. Let us look at the "freedom of conscience and worship" in England under that irreverent Defender of the Faith, Charles II. Ellwood says: "He that commanded the party gave us first a general charge to come out of the room. But we, who came thither at God's requiring to worship Him (like that good man of old, who said, *we ought to obey God rather than man*), stirred not, but kept our places. Whereupon, he sent some of his soldiers among us, with command to drag or drive us out, which they did roughly enough." Think of it: grave men and women, and modest maidens, sitting there with calm, impassive countenances, motionless as death, the pikes of the soldiery closing about them in a circle of bristling steel! Brave and true ones! Not in vain did ye thus oppose God's silence to the Devil's uproar; Christian endurance and calm persistence in the exercise of your rights as Englishmen and men to the hot fury of impatient tyranny! From your day down to this, the world has been the better for your faithfulness.

Ellwood and some thirty of his friends were marched off to prison in Old Bridewell, which, as well as nearly all the other prisons, was already crowded with Quaker prisoners. One of the rooms of the prison was used as a torture chamber. "I was almost affrighted," says Ellwood, "by the dismalness of the place; for, besides that the walls were all laid over with black, from top to bottom, there stood in the middle a great whipping-post.

"The manner of whipping there is, to strip the party to the skin, from the waist upward, and, having fastened him to the whipping-post (so that he can neither resist nor shun the strokes), to lash his naked body with long, slender twigs of holly, which will bend almost like thongs around the body; and these, having little knots upon them, tear the skin and flesh, and give extreme pain."

To this terrible punishment aged men and delicately nurtured young females were often subjected, during this season of hot persecution.

From the Bridewell, Ellwood was at length removed to Newgate, and thrust in, with other "Friends," amid the common felons. He speaks of this prison, with its thieves, murderers, and prostitutes, its over-crowded apartments, and loathsome cells, as "a hell upon earth." In a closet, adjoining the room where he was lodged, lay for several days the quartered bodies of Phillips, Tongue, and Gibbs, the leaders of the Fifth Monarchy rising, frightful and loathsome, as they came from the bloody hands of the executioners! These ghastly remains were at length obtained by the friends of the dead, and buried. The heads were ordered to be prepared for setting up in different parts of the city. Read this grim passage of description:

"I saw the heads when they were brought to be boiled. The hangman fetched them in a dirty basket, out of some by-place, and setting them down among the felons, he and they made sport of them. They took them by the hair, flouting, jeering, and laughing at them; and then, giving them some ill names, boxed them on their ears and cheeks; which done, the hangman put them into his kettle, and parboiled them with bay salt and cummin seed: *that* to keep them from putrefaction, and *this* to keep off the fowls from seizing upon them. The whole sight, as well that of the bloody quarters first, as this of the heads afterward, was both frightful and loathsome, and begat an abhorrence in my nature."

At the next session of the municipal court at the Old Bailey, Ellwood obtained his discharge. After paying a visit to "my Master Milton," he made his way to Chalfont, the home of his friends the Penningtons, where he was soon after engaged as a Latin teacher. Here he seems to have had his trials and temptations. Gulielma Springette, the daughter of Pennington's wife, his old playmate, had now grown to be "a fair woman of marriageable age," and, as he informs us, "very desirable, whether regard was had to her outward person, which wanted nothing to make her completely comely, or to the endowments of her mind, which were every way extraordinary, or to her outward fortune, which was fair." From all which, we are not surprised to learn that "she was secretly and openly sought for by many of almost every rank and condition." "To whom," continues Thomas, "in their respective turns (till he at length came for whom she was reserved), she carried herself with so much evenness of temper, such courteous freedom, guarded by the strictest modesty, that as it gave encouragement or ground of hope to none, so neither did it administer any matter of offense or just cause of complaint to any."

Beautiful and noble maiden! How the imagination fills up this outline lining by her friend, and, if truth must be told, admirer! Serene, courteous, healthful; a ray of tenderest and blandest light, shining steadily in the sober gloom of that old household! Confirmed Quaker as she is, shrinking from none of the responsibilities and dangers of her profession, and therefore liable at any time to the penalties of prison and whipping-post, under that plain garb and in spite of that "certain gravity of look and behavior," which, as we have seen, on one occasion awed young Ellwood into silence, youth, beauty, and refinement assert their prerogatives; love knows no creed; the gay, and titled, and wealthy crowd around her, suing in vain for her favor.

> Followed, like the tided moon,
> She moves as calmly on,

"Until he at length comes for whom she was reserved," and her name is united with that of one worthy even of her, the world-renowned William Penn.

Meantime, one cannot but feel a good degree of sympathy with young Ellwood, her old schoolmate and playmate, placed, as he was, in the same family with her, enjoying her familiar conversation and unreserved confidence; and, as he says, the "advantageous opportunities of riding and walking abroad with her, by night as well as by day, without any other company than her maid; for so great, indeed, was the confidence that her mother had in me, that she thought her daughter safe, if I was with her, even from the plots and designs of others upon her." So near, and yet, alas! in truth, so distant! The serene and gentle light which shone upon him, in the sweet solitudes of Chalfont, was that of a star, itself unapproachable. As he himself meekly intimates, she was reserved for another. He seems to have fully understood his own position in respect to her; although, to use his own words, "others, measuring him by the propensity of their own inclinations, concluded he would steal her, run away with her, and marry her." Little did these jealous surmisers know of the true and really heroic spirit of the young Latin master. His own apology and defense of his conduct, under circumstances of temptation which St. Anthony himself could have scarcely better resisted, will not be amiss:

"I was not ignorant of the various fears which filled the jealous heads of some concerning me, neither was I so stupid nor so divested of all humanity as not to be sensible of the real and innate worth and virtue which adorned that excellent dame, and attracted the eyes and hearts of so many, with the greatest importunity, to seek and solicit her; nor was I so devoid of natural heat as not to feel some sparklings of desire, as well as others; but the force of truth and sense of honor suppressed whatever would have risen beyond the bounds of fair and virtuous friendship. For I easily foresaw, that, if I should have attempted anything in a dishonorable way, by fraud or force, upon her, I should have thereby brought a wound upon mine own soul, a foul scandal upon my religious profession, and an infamous stain upon mine honor, which was far more dear unto me than my life. Wherefore, having observed how some others had befooled themselves, by misconstruing her common kindness (expressed in an innocent, open, free, and familiar conversation, springing from the abundant affability, courtesy, and sweetness of her natural temper) to be the effect of a singular regard and peculiar affection to them, I resolved to shun the rock whereon they split; and, remembering the saying of the poet,

> Felix quem faciunt aliena Pericula cantum,

I governed myself in a free yet respectful carriage toward her, thereby preserving a fair reputation with my friends, and enjoying as much of her favor and kindness, in a virtuous and firm friendship, as was fit for her to show or for me to seek."

Well and worthily said, poor Thomas! Whatever might be said of others, thou, at least, wast no coxcomb. Thy distant and involuntary admiration of "the fair Guli" needs, however, no excuse. Poor human nature, guard it as one may, with strictest discipline and painfully cramping environment, will sometimes act out itself; and, in thy case, not even George Fox himself, knowing thy beautiful young friend (and doubtless admiring her too, for he was one of the first to appreciate and honor the worth and dignity of woman), could have found it in his heart to censure thee!

At this period, as was indeed most natural, our young teacher solaced himself with occasional appeals to what he calls "the Muses." There is reason to believe, however, that the Pagan sisterhood whom he ventured to invoke seldom graced his study with their personal attendance. In these rhyming efforts, scattered up and down his Journal, there are occasional sparkles of genuine wit, and passages of keen sarcasm, tersely and fitly expressed. Others breathe a warm, devotional feeling; in the following brief prayer, for instance, the wants of the humble Christian are condensed in a manner worthy of Quarles or Herbert:

> Oh! that mine eye might closed be
> To what concerns me not to see;
> That deafness might possess mine ear
> To what concerns me not to hear;
> That Truth my tongue might always tie
> From ever speaking foolishly;

That no vain thought might ever rest
Or be conceived in my breast;
That by each word and deed and thought,
Glory may to my God be brought!
But what are wishes? Lord, mine eye
On Thee is fixed, to Thee I cry:
Wash, Lord, and purify my heart,
And make it clean in every part;
And when 'tis clean, Lord, keep it too,
For that is more than I can do.

The thought in the following extracts, from a poem, written on the death of his friend Pennington's son, is trite, but not inaptly or inelegantly expressed:

What ground, alas, has any man
  To set his heart on things below,
Which, when they seem most like to stand,
  Fly like the arrow from the bow!
Who's now atop ere long shall feel
The circling motion of the wheel!

The world cannot afford a thing
  Which to a well-composed mind
Can any lasting pleasure bring,
  But in itself its grave will find.
All things unto their center tend—
What had beginning must have end!

No disappointment can befall
  Us, having Him who's all in all!
What can of pleasure him prevent
Who hath the Fountain of Content?

In the year 1663 a severe law was enacted against the "sect called Quakers," prohibiting their meetings, with the penalty of banishment for the third offense! The burden of the prosecution which followed fell upon the Quakers of the metropolis, large numbers of whom were heavily fined, imprisoned, and sentenced to be banished from their native land. Yet, in time, our worthy friend Ellwood came in for his own share of trouble, in consequence of attending the funeral of one of his friends. An evil-disposed justice of the county obtained information of the Quaker gathering; and while the body of the dead was "borne on Friends' shoulders through the street, in order to be carried to the burying-ground, which was at the town's end," says Ellwood, "he rushed out upon us with the constables and a rabble of rude fellows whom he had gathered together, and having his drawn sword in his hand, struck one of the foremost of the bearers with it, commanding them to set down the coffin. But the Friend who was so stricken, being more concerned for the safety of the dead body than for his own, lest it should fall, and any indecency thereupon follow, held the coffin fast; which the justice observing, and being enraged that his word was not forthwith obeyed, set his hand to the coffin, and with a forcible thrust threw it off from the bearers' shoulders, so that it fell to the ground in the middle of the street, and there we were forced to leave it; for the constables and rabble fell upon us, and drew some and drove others into the inn. Of those thus taken," continues Ellwood, "I was one. They picked out ten of us, and sent us to Aylesbury jail."

"They caused the body to lie in the open street and cartway, so that all travelers that passed, whether horsemen, coaches, carts, or wagons, were fain to break out of the way to go by it, until it was almost night. And then, having caused a grave to be made in the *unconsecrated* part of what is called the Church-yard, they forcibly took the body from the widow, and buried it there."

He remained a prisoner only about two months, during which period he comforted himself by such verse-making as follows, reminding us of similar enigmas in Bunyan's Pilgrim's Progress:

Lo! a Riddle for the wise,
In the which a Mystery lies.

RIDDLE.

Some men are free whilst they in prison lie;
Others who ne'er saw prison, captives die.

CAUTION.

He that can receive it may.
He that cannot, let him stay;
Not be hasty, but suspend
Judgment till he sees the end.

SOLUTION.

He's only free indeed, who's free from sin,
And he is fastest bound, that's bound therein.

In the mean time, where is our "Master Milton"? We left him deprived of his young companion and reader, sitting lonely in his small dining-room in Jewen Street. It is now the year 1665; is not the pestilence in London? A sinful and godless city, with its bloated bishops, fawning around the Nell Gwynns of a licentious and profane Defender of the Faith; its swaggering and drunken cavaliers; its ribald jesters; its obscene ballad-singers: its loathsome prisons, crowded with God-fearing men and women; is not the measure of its iniquity already filled up? Three years only have passed since the terrible prayer of Vane went upward from the scaffold on Tower Hill: "When my blood is shed upon the block, let it, oh God, have a voice afterward!" Audible to thy ear, oh bosom friend of the martyr! has that blood cried from earth; and now, how fearfully is it answered! Like the ashes which the Seer of the Hebrews cast toward Heaven, it has returned in boils and blains upon the proud and oppressive city. John Milton, sitting blind in Jewen Street, has heard the toll of the death bells, and the night-long rumble of the burial-carts, and the terrible summons, "BRING OUT YOUR DEAD!" The Angel of the Plague, in yellow mantle, purple-spotted, walks the streets. Why should he tarry in a doomed city, forsaken of God! Is not the command, even to him, "Arise! and flee for thy life." In some green nook of the quiet country, he may finish the great work which his hands have found to do. He bethinks him of his old friends, the Penningtons, and his young Quaker companion, the patient and gentle Ellwood. "Wherefore," says the latter, "some little time before I went to Aylesbury jail, I was desired by my quondam Master Milton to take an house for him in the neighborhood where I dwelt, that he might go out of the city for the safety of himself and his family, the pestilence then growing hot in London. I took a pretty box for him in Giles Chalfont, a mile from me, of which I gave him notice, and intended to have waited on him and seen him well settled, but was prevented by that imprisonment. But now, being released and returned home, I soon made a visit to him, to welcome him into the country. After some common discourse had passed between us, he called for a manuscript of his, which having brought, he delivered to me, bidding me take it home with me and read it at my leisure, and when I had so done, return it to him with my judgment thereupon."

Now, what does the reader think young Ellwood carried in his gray coat pocket across the dikes and hedges and through the green lanes of Giles Chalfont that autumn day? Let us look farther: "When I came home, and had set myself to read it, I found it was that excellent poem which he entitled Paradise Lost. After I had, with the best attention, read it through, I made him another visit; and returning his book with due acknowledgment of the favor he had done me in communicating it to me, he asked me how I liked it, and what I thought of it, which I modestly but freely told him; and, after some farther discourse about it, I pleasantly said to him, 'Thou hast said much here of Paradise *Lost;* what hast thou to say of Paradise *Found?*' He made me no answer, but sat some time in a muse, then brake off that discourse, and fell upon another subject."

"I modestly but freely told him what I thought" of Paradise Lost! What he told him remains a mystery. One would like to know more precisely what the first critical reader of that song of "Man's first disobedience" thought of it. Fancy the young Quaker and blind Milton sitting some pleasant afternoon of the autumn of that old year, in "the pretty box" at Chalfont, the soft wind through the open window lifting the thin hair of the glorious old poet! Backslidden England, plague-smitten, and accursed with her faithless Church and libertine king, knows little of poor "Master Milton," and takes small note of his puritanic verse-making. Alone, with his humble friend, he sits there, conning over that poem which, he fondly hoped the world, which had grown all dark and strange to the author, "would not willingly let die." The suggestion in respect to Paradise Found, to which, as we have seen, "he made no answer, but sat some time in a muse," seems not to have been lost; for, "after the sickness was over," continues Ellwood, "and the city well cleansed, and become safely habitable again, he returned thither; and when afterward I waited on him there, which I seldom failed of doing whenever my occasions drew me to London, he showed me his second poem, called Paradise Gained; and, in a pleasant tone, said to me, 'This is owing to you, for you put it into my head by the question you put to me at Chalfont, which before I had not thought of."

Golden days were these for the young Latin reader, even if it be true, as we suspect, that he was himself very far from appreciating the glorious privilege which he enjoyed, of the familiar friendship and confidence of Milton. But they could not last. His amiable host, Isaac Pennington, a blameless and quiet country gentleman, was dragged from his house by a military force, and lodged in Aylesbury jail; his wife and family forcibly ejected from their pleasant home, which was seized upon by the government as security for the fines imposed upon its owner. The plague was in the village of Aylesbury, and in the very prison itself; but the noble-hearted Mary Pennington followed her husband, sharing with him the dark peril. Poor Ellwood, while attending a monthly meeting at Hedgerly, with six others (among them one Morgan Watkins, a poor old Welshman, who, painfully endeavoring to utter his testimony in his own dialect, was suspected by the Dogberry of a justice of being a Jesuit trolling over his Latin), was arrested, and committed to Wiccomb House of Correction.

This was a time of severe trial for the sect with which Ellwood had connected himself. In the very midst of the pestilence, when thousands perished weekly in London, fifty-four Quakers were marched through the almost deserted streets, and placed on board a ship, for the purpose of being conveyed, according to their sentence of banishment, to the West Indies. The ship lay for a long time, with many others similarly situated, a helpless prey to the pestilence. Through that terrible autumn, the prisoners sat waiting for the summons of the ghastly Destroyer; and, from their floating dungeon,

> Heard the groan
> Of agonizing ships from shore to shore;
> Heard nightly plunged beneath the sullen wave
> The frequent corse.

When the vessel at length set sail, of the fifty-four who went on board, twenty-seven only were living. A Dutch privateer captured her when two days out, and carried the prisoners to North Holland, where they were set at liberty. The condition of the jails in the city, where were large numbers of Quakers, was dreadful in the extreme. Ill ventilated, crowded, and loathsome with the accumulated filth of centuries, they invited the disease which daily decimated their cells. "Go on!" says Pennington, writing to the king and bishops from his plague-infected cell in the Aylesbury prison, "try it out with the Spirit of the Lord, come forth with your laws, and prisons, and spoiling of goods, and banishment, and death, if the Lord please, and see if ye can carry it! Whom the Lord loveth, He can save at His pleasure. Hath He begun to break our bonds and deliver us, and shall we now distrust Him? Are we in a worse condition than Israel was when the sea was before them, the mountains on either side, and the Egyptians behind pursuing them?"

Brave men and faithful! It is not necessary that the present generation, now quietly reaping the fruit of your heroic endurance, should see eye to eye with you in respect to all your testimonies and beliefs, in order to recognize your claim to gratitude and admiration. For, in an age of hypocritical hollowness and mean self-seeking, when, with noble exceptions, the very Puritans of Cromwell's Reign of the Saints were taking profane lessons from their old enemies, and putting on an outside show of conformity for the sake of place or pardon, ye maintained the austere dignity of virtue, and, with King and Church and Parliament arrayed against you, vindicated the Rights of conscience, at the cost of home, fortune, and life. English liberty owes more to your unyielding firmness than to the blows stricken for her at Worcester and Naseby.

In 1667, we find the Latin teacher in attendance at a great meeting of Friends in London, convened, at the suggestion of George Fox, for the purpose of settling a little difficulty which had arisen among the Friends, even under the pressure of the severest persecution, relative to the very important matter of "wearing the hat." George Fox, in his love of truth and sincerity, in word and action, had discountenanced the fashionable doffing of the hat, and other flattering obeisances toward men holding stations in Church or State, as savoring of man-worship, giving to the creature the reverence only due to the Creator, as undignified and wanting in due self-respect, and tending to support unnatural and oppressive distinctions among those equal in the sight of God. But some of his disciples evidently made much more of this "hat testimony" than their teacher. One John Perrott, who had just returned from an unsuccessful attempt to convert the Pope, at Rome (where that dignitary, after listening to his exhortations, and finding him in no condition to be benefited by the spiritual physicians of the Inquisition, had quietly turned him over to the temporal ones of the Insane Hospital), had broached the doctrine that, in public or private worship, the hat was not to be taken off without an immediate revelation or call to do so! Ellwood himself seems to have been on the point of yielding to this notion, which appears to have been the occasion of a good deal of dissension and scandal. Under these circumstances, to save truth from reproach, and an important testimony to the essential equality of mankind from running into sheer fanaticism, Fox summoned his tried and faithful friends together, from all parts of the United Kingdom, and, as it appears, with the happiest result. Hat-revelations were discountenanced, good order and harmony re-established, and John Perrott's beaver, and the crazy head under it, were from thenceforth powerless for evil. Let those who are disposed to laugh at this notable Ecumenical Council of the Hat, consider that ecclesiastical history has brought down to us the records of many larger and more imposing convocations, wherein grave bishops and learned fathers took each other by the beard upon matters of far less practical importance.

In 1669, we find Ellwood engaged in escorting his

fair friend, Gulielma, to her uncle's residence in Sussex. Passing through London, and taking the Tunbridge road, they stopped at Seven Oak to dine. The Duke of York was on the road, with his guards and hangers-on, and the inn was filled with a rude company. "Hastening," says Ellwood, "from a place where we found nothing but rudeness, the roysterers who swarmed there, besides the damning oaths they belched out against each other, looked very sourly upon us, as if they grudged us the horses which we rode and the clothes we wore." They had proceeded but a little distance, when they were overtaken by some half-dozen drunken rough-riding cavaliers, of the Wildrake stamp, in full pursuit after the beautiful Quakeress. One of them impudently attempted to pull her upon his horse before him, but was held at bay by Ellwood, who seems, on this occasion, to have relied somewhat upon his "stick," in defending his fair charge. Calling up Gulielma's servant, he bade him ride on one side of his mistress, while he guarded her on the other. "But he," says Ellwood, "not thinking it perhaps decent to ride so near his mistress, left room enough for another to ride between." In dashed the drunken retainer, and Gulielma was once more in peril. It was clearly no time for exhortations and expostulations, "So," says Ellwood, "I chopped in upon him, by a nimble turn, and kept him at bay. I told him I had hitherto spared him, but wished him not to provoke me further. This I spoke in such a tone as bespoke an high resentment of the abuse put upon us, and withal, pressed him so hard with my horse, that I suffered him not to come up again to Guli." By this time, it became evident to the companions of the ruffianly assailant that the young Quaker was in earnest, and they hastened to interfere. "For they," says Ellwood, "seeing the contest rise so high, and probably fearing it would rise higher, not knowing where it might stop, came in to part us; which they did, by taking him away."

Escaping from these sons of Belial, Ellwood and his fair companion rode on through Tunbridge Wells, "the street thronged with men, who looked very earnestly at them, but offered them no affront," and arrived, late at night, in a driving rain, at the mansion house of Herbert Springette. The fiery old gentleman was so indignant at the insult offered to his niece, that he was with difficulty dissuaded from demanding satisfaction at the hands of the Duke of York.

This seems to have been his last ride with Gulielma. She was soon after married to William Penn, and took up her abode at Worminghurst, in Sussex. How blessed and beautiful was that union may be understood from the following paragraph of a letter, written by her husband, on the eve of his departure for America to lay the foundations of a Christian colony.

"My dear wife, remember thou wast the love of my youth, and much the joy of my life; the most beloved, as well as the most worthy of all my earthly comforts; and the reason of that love was more thy inward than thy outward excellences, which yet were many. God knows, and thou knowest it, I can say it was a match of Providence's making and God's image in us both was the first thing and the most amiable and engaging ornament in our eyes."

About this time, our friend Thomas, seeing that his old playmate at Chalfont was destined for another, turned his attention toward a "young Friend, named Mary Ellis." He had been for several years acquainted with her, but now he "found his heart secretly drawn and inclining toward her." "At length," he tells us, "as I was sitting all alone, waiting upon the Lord for counsel and guidance in this, in itself and to me, important affair, I felt a word sweetly arise in me, as if I had heard a voice which said, *Go, and prevail!* and Faith springing in my heart at the word, I immediately rose and went, nothing doubting." On arriving at her residence, he states that he "solemnly opened his mind to her, which was a great surprisal to her, for she had taken in an apprehension, as others had also done," that his eye had been fixed elsewhere and nearer home. "I used not many words to her," he continues, "but I felt a Divine Power went along with the words, and fixed the matter expressed by them so fast in her breast, that, as she afterward acknowledged to me, she could not shut it out."

"I continued," he says, "my visits to my best beloved Friend until we married, which was on the 28th day of the eighth month, 1669. We took each other in a select meeting of the ancient and grave Friends of that country. A very solemn meeting it was and in a weighty frame of spirit we were." His wife seems to have had some estate; and Ellwood, with that nice sense of justice which marked all his actions, immediately made his will, securing to her, in case of his decease, all her own goods and moneys as well as all that he had himself acquired before marriage. "Which," he tells, "was indeed but little, yet by all that little, more than I had ever given her ground to expect with me." His father, who was yet unreconciled to the son's religious views, found fault with his marriage on the ground that it was unlawful and unsanctioned by priest or liturgy, and consequently refused to render him any pecuniary assistance. Yet in spite of this and other trials, he seems to have preserved his serenity of spirit. After an unpleasant interview with his father, on one occasion, he wrote, at his lodgings in an inn, in London, what he calls "A song of Praise." An extract from it will serve to show the spirit of the good man in affliction:

Unto the glory of Thy Holy Name,
  Eternal God! whom I both love and fear,
I hereby do declare, I never came
  Before Thy throne, and found Thee loth to hear,
  But always ready with an open ear,
And though, sometimes, Thou seem'st Thy face to hide,
  As one that had withdrawn his love from me,
'Tis that my faith may to the full be tried,
  And that I thereby may the better see
  How weak I am when not upheld by Thee!

The next year, 1670, an act of Parliament, in relation to "Conventicles," provided that any person who should be present at any meeting, under color or pretense of any exercise of religion, in other manner than according to the liturgy and practice of the Church of England "should be liable to fines of from five to ten shillings; and any person preaching at or giving his house for the meeting, to a fine of twenty pounds; one-third of the fines being received by the informer or informers." As a natural consequence of such a law, the vilest scoundrels in the land set up the trade of informers and heresy-hunters.

Wherever a dissenting meeting or burial took place, there was sure to be a mercenary spy, ready to bring a complaint against all in attendance. The Independents and Baptists ceased, in a great measure, to hold public meetings, yet even they did not escape prosecution. Bunyan, for instance, in these days, was dreaming, like another Jacob, of angels ascending and descending, in Bedford prison. But upon the poor Quakers fell, as usual, the great force of the unjust enactment. Some of these spies or informers, men of sharp wit, close countenances, pliant tempers, and skill in dissimulation, took the guise of Quakers, Independents, or Baptists as occasion required, thrusting themselves into the meetings of the proscribed sects, ascertaining the number who attended, their rank and condition, and then informing against them. Ellwood, in his journal for 1670, describes several of these emissaries of evil. One of them came to a Friend's house, in Bucks, professing to be a brother in the faith, but, overdoing his counterfeit Quakerism, was detected and dismissed by his host. Betaking himself to the inn, he appeared in his true character, drank and swore roundly, and confessed over his cups that he had been sent forth on his mission by the Rev. Dr. Mew, Vice-Chancelor of Oxford. Finding little success in counterfeiting Quakerism, he turned to the Baptists, where, for a time, he met with better success. Ellwood, at this time, rendered good service to his friends, by exposing the true character of these wretches, and bringing them to justice for theft, perjury, and other misdemeanors.

While this storm of persecution lasted (a period of two or three years), the different dissenting sects felt, in some measure, a common sympathy, and, while guarding themselves against their common foe, had little leisure for controversy with each other; but as was natural, the abatement of their mutual suffering and danger was the signal for renewing their suspended quarrels. The Baptists fell upon the Quakers, with pamphlet and sermon; the latter replied in the same way. One of the most conspicuous of the Baptist disputants was the famous Jeremy Ives, with whom our friend Ellwood seems to have had a good deal of trouble. "His name," says Ellwood, "was up for a topping disputant. He was well read in the fallacies of logic, and was ready in framing syllogisms. His chief art lay in tickling the humor of rude, unlearned, and injudicious hearers."

The following piece of Ellwood's, entitled "An Epitaph for Jeremy Ives," will serve to show that wit and drollery were sometimes found even among the proverbially sober Quakers of the seventeenth century:

Beneath this stone, depressed doth lie
The mirror of Hypocrisy—
Ives, whose mercenary tongue
Like a weathercock was hung,
And did this or that way play,
As Advantage led the way.
If well hired, he would dispute,
Otherwise he would be mute.
But he'd bawl for half a day,
If he knew and liked his pay.

For his person, let it pass;
Only note his face was brass.
His heart was like a pumice stone,
And for conscience he had none.
Of *earth* and *air* he was composed,
With *water* round about inclosed.
Earth in him had greatest share,
Questionless, his life lay there;
Thence his cankered envy sprung,
Poisoning both his heart and tongue.

Air made him frothy, light, and vain,
And puffed him with a proud disdain.
Into the water oft he went,
And through the water many sent,
That was, ye know, his element!
The greatest odds that did appear
Was this, for aught that I can hear,
That he in *cold* did others dip,
But did himself *hot* water sip.

And his cause he'd never doubt,
If well soak'd o'er night in stout;
But, meanwhile, he must not lack
Brandy, and a draught of sack.
One dispute would shrink a bottle
Of three pints, if not a pottle.
One would think he fetched from thence
All his dreamy eloquence.

Let us now bring back the sot
To his aqua vita pot,
And observe, with some content,
How he framed his argument.
That his whistle he might wet,
The bottle to his mouth he set,
And being master of that art,
Thence he drew the *major* part,
But left the *minor* still behind;
Good reason why, he wanted wind;
If his breath would have held out,
He had *conclusion* drawn, no doubt.

The residue of Ellwood's life seems to have glided on in serenity and peace. He wrote, at intervals, many pamphlets in defense of his society, and in favor of liberty of conscience. At his hospitable residence, the leading spirits of the sect were warmly welcomed. George Fox and William Penn seem to have been frequent guests. We find that, in 1683, he was arrested for seditious publications, when on the eve of hastening to his early friend, Gulielma, who, in the absence of her husband, Governor Penn, had fallen dangerously ill. On coming before the judge, "I told him," says Ellwood, "that I had that morning received an express out of Sussex, that William Penn's wife (with whom I had an intimate acquaintance and strict friendship, *ab ipsis fere incunabilis*, at least, *a teneris unguiculis*) lay now ill, not without great danger, and that she had expressed her desire that I would come to her as soon as I could." The judge said, "He was very sorry for Madam Penn's illness," of whose virtues he spoke very highly, but not more than was her due. Then he told me, "that for her sake he would do what he could to further my visit to her." Escaping from the hands of the law, he visited his friend, who was by this time in a way of recovery, and, on his return, learned that the prosecution had been abandoned.

At about this date his narrative ceases. We learn, from other sources, that he continued to write and print in defense of his religious views up to the year of his death, which took place in 1713. One of his productions, a poetical version of the life of David, may be still met with, in the old Quaker libraries. On the score of poetical merit, it is about on a level with Michael Drayton's verses on the same subject. As the history of one of the firm confessors of the old struggle for religious freedom, of a genial-hearted and pleasant scholar, the friend of Penn and Milton, and the suggester of Paradise Regained, we trust our hurried sketch has not been altogether without interest; and that, whatever may be the religious views of our readers, they have not failed to recognize a good and true man in Thomas Ellwood.

JAMES NAYLER.

You will here read the true story of that much injured, ridiculed man, James Nayler; what dreadful sufferings, with what patience he endured, even to the boring of the tongue with hot irons, without a murmur; and with what strength of mind, when the delusion he had fallen into, which they stigmatized as blasphemy, had given place to clearer thoughts, he could renounce his error in a strain of the beautifullest humility.—*Essays of Elia.*

"WOULD that Carlyle could now try his hand at the English revolution!" was our exclamation, on laying down the last volume of his remarkable "History of the French Revolution," with its brilliant and startling word-pictures still flashing before us. To some extent this wish has been realized in the "Letters and Speeches of Oliver Cromwell." Yet we confess that the perusal of these volumes has disappointed us. Instead of giving himself free scope, as in his French Revolution, and transferring to his canvas all the wild and ludicrous, the terrible and beautiful phases of that moral phenomenon, he has here concentrated all his artistic skill upon a single figure, whom he seems to have regarded as the embodiment and hero of the great event. All else on his canvas is subordinated to the grim image of the colossal Puritan. Intent upon presenting him as the fitting object of that "Hero-worship," which, in its blind admiration and adoration of mere abstract Power, seems to us at times nothing less than Devil-worship, he dwarfs, casts into the shadow, nay, in some instances, caricatures and distorts the figures which surround him. To excuse Cromwell in his usurpation, Henry Vane, one of those exalted and noble characters, upon whose features the lights held by historical friends or foes detect no blemish, is dismissed with a sneer, and an utterly unfounded imputation of dishonesty. To reconcile, in some degree, the discrepancy between the declarations of Cromwell in behalf of freedom of conscience, and that mean and cruel persecution which the Quakers suffered under the Protectorate, the generally harmless fanaticism of a few individuals, bearing that name, is gravely urged. Nay, the fact that some weak-brained enthusiasts undertook to bring about the Millennium, by associating together, cultivating the earth, and "dibbling beans" for the New-Jerusalem market, is regarded by our author as the "germ of Quakerism"; and furnishes an occasion for sneering at "my poor friend Dry-as-dust, lamentably tearing his hair over the intolerance of that old time to Quakerism and such like."

The readers of this (with all its faults) powerfully written Biography cannot fail to have been impressed with the intensely graphic description (Part I, vol. ii, pages 184, 185) of the entry of the poor fanatic, James Nayler, and his forlorn and draggled companions into Bristol. Sadly ludicrous is it; affecting us like the actual sight of tragic insanity enacting its involuntary comedy, and making us smile through our tears.

In another portion of the work, a brief account is given of the trial and sentence of Nayler, also in the serio-comic view; and the poor man is dismissed with the simple intimation, that after his punishment, he "repented, and confessed himself mad." It was no part of the author's business, we are well aware, to waste time and words upon the history of such a man as Nayler; he was of no importance to him, otherwise than as one of the disturbing influences in the government of the Lord Protector. But in our mind the story of James Nayler has always been one of interest; and in the belief that it will prove so to others, who, like Charles Lamb, can appreciate the beautiful humility of a forgiving spirit, we have taken some pains to collect and embody the facts of it.

James Nayler was born in the parish of Ardesley, in Yorkshire, 1616. His father was a substantial farmer, of good repute and competent estate; and he, in consequence, received a good education. At the age of twenty-two he married and removed to Wakefield parish, which has since been made classic ground by the pen of Goldsmith. Here, an honest, God-fearing farmer, he tilled his soil, and alternated between cattle-markets and Independent conventicles. In 1641 he obeyed the summons of "my Lord Fairfax" and the Parliament, and joined a troop of horse composed of sturdy Independents, doing such signal service against "the man of Belial,

Charles Stuart," that he was promoted to the rank of quartermaster, in which capacity he served under General Lambert, in his Scottish campaign. Disabled at length by sickness, he was honorably dismissed from the service, and returned to his family in 1649.

For three or four years he continued to attend the meetings of the Independents as a zealous and devout member. But it so fell out that, in the winter of 1651, George Fox, who had just been released from a cruel imprisonment in Derby jail, felt a call to set his face toward Yorkshire. "So traveling," says Fox in his journal, "through the countries, to several places, preaching Repentance and the Word of Life, I came into the parts about Wakefield where James Nayler lived." The worn and weary soldier, covered with the scars of outward battle, received, as he believed, in the cause of God and his people, against Antichrist and oppression, welcomed with thankfulness the veteran of another warfare, who, in conflict with "principalities and powers, and spiritual wickedness in high places," had made his name a familiar one in every English hamlet. "He and Thomas Goodyear," says Fox, "came to me, and were both convinced, and received the truth." He soon after joined the Society of Friends. In the spring of the next year he was in his field following his plow, and meditating, as he was wont, on the great questions of life and duty, when he seemed to hear a voice bidding him go out from his kindred and his father's house, with an assurance that the Lord would be with him while laboring in his service. Deeply impressed, he left his employment, and, returning to his house, made immediate preparations for a journey. But hesitation and doubt followed; he became sick from anxiety of mind, and his recovery, for a time, was exceedingly doubtful. On his restoration to bodily health, he obeyed what he regarded as a clear intimation of duty, and went forth a preacher of the doctrines he had embraced. The Independent minister of the society to which he had formerly belonged sent after him the story that he was the victim of sorcery; that George Fox carried with him a bottle, out of which he made people drink; and that the draught had the power to change a Presbyterian or Independent into a Quaker at once; that, in short, the Arch-Quaker, Fox, was a wizard, and could be seen at the same moment of time, riding on the same black horse, in two places widely separated! He had scarcely commenced his exhortations, before the mob, excited by such stories, assailed him. In the early summer of the year we hear of him in Appleby jail. On his release, he fell in company with George Fox. At Walney Island he was furiously assaulted and beaten with clubs and stones, the poor priest-led fishermen being fully persuaded that they were dealing with a wizard. The spirit of the man, under these circumstances, may be seen in the following extract from a letter to his friends, dated at "Killet, in Lancashire, the 30th of 8th Month, 1652."

"Dear friends! Dwell in patience, and wait upon the Lord, who will do his own work. Look not at man who is in the work, nor at any man opposing it; but rest in the will of the Lord, that so ye may be furnished with patience, both to do and to suffer what ye shall be called unto, that your end in all things may be His praise. Meet often together; take heed of what exalteth itself above its brother; but keep low, and serve one another in love."

Laboring thus, interrupted only by persecution, stripes, and imprisonment, he finally came to London, and spoke with great power and eloquence in the meetings of Friends in that city. Here he for the first time found himself surrounded by admiring and sympathizing friends. He saw and rejoiced in the fruits of his ministry. Profane and drunken cavaliers, intolerant Presbyters, and blind Papists owned the truths which he uttered, and counted themselves his disciples. Women, too, in their deep trustfulness, and admiring reverence, sat at the feet of the eloquent stranger. Devout believers in the doctrine of the inward light and manifestation of God in the heart of man, these latter, at length, thought they saw such unmistakable evidences of the true life in James Nayler, that they felt constrained to declare that Christ was, in an especial manner, within him, and to call upon all to recognize in reverent adoration this new incarnation of the divine and heavenly. The wild enthusiasm of his disciples had its effect on the teacher. Weak in body, worn with sickness, fasting, stripes, and prison penance, and naturally credulous and imaginative, is it strange that in some measure he yielded to this miserable delusion? Let those who would harshly judge him, or ascribe his fall to the peculiar doctrines of his sect, think of Luther, engaged in personal combat with the devil, or conversing with him on points of theology in his bedchamber; or of Bunyan at actual fisticuffs with the adversary; or of Fleetwood and Vane and Harrison millennium-mad, and making preparations for an earthly reign of King Jesus. It was an age of intense religious excitement. Fanaticism had become epidemic. Cromwell swayed his parliaments by "revelations" and Scripture phrases in the painted chamber; stout generals and sea-captains exterminated the Irish, and swept Dutch navies from the ocean, with old Jewish war-cries, and hymns of Deborah and Miriam; country justices charged juries in Hebraisms, and cited the laws of Palestine oftener than those of England. Poor Nayler found himself in the very midst of this seething and confused moral mäelstrom. He struggled against it for a time, but human nature was weak; he became, to use his own words, "bewildered and darkened," and the floods went over him.

Leaving London with some of his more zealous followers, not without solemn admonition and rebuke from Francis Howgill and Edward Burrough, who at that period were regarded as the most eminent and gifted of the Society's ministers, he bent his steps toward Exeter. Here, in consequence of the extravagance of his language and that of his disciples, he was arrested and thrown into prison. Several infatuated women surrounded the jail, declaring that "Christ was in prison," and on being admitted to see him knelt down and kissed his feet, exclaiming, "Thy name shall be no more called James Nayler, but Jesus!" Let us pity him and them. They, full of grateful and extravagant affection for the man whose voice had called them away from worldly vanities to what they regarded as eternal realities, whose hand they imagined had for them swung back the pearl gates of the celestial city, and flooded their atmosphere with light from heaven; he, receiving their homage (not as offered to a poor, weak, sinful Yorkshire trooper, but rather to the hidden man of the heart, the "Christ within" him) with that self-deceiving humility which is but another name for spiritual pride. Mournful, yet natural; such as is still in greater or less degree manifested between the Catholic enthusiast and her confessor; such as the careful observer may at times take note of in our Protestant revivals and camp meetings.

How Nayler was released from Exeter jail does not appear, but the next we hear of him is at Bristol, in the fall of the year. His entrance into that city shows the progress which he and his followers had made in the interval. Let us look at Carlyle's description of it. "A procession of eight persons—one, a man on horseback, riding single; the others, men and women, partly riding double, partly on foot, in the muddiest highway in the wettest weather; singing, all but the single rider, at whose bridle walk and splash two women, 'Hosannah! Holy, holy! Lord God of Sabaoth,' and other things, 'in a buzzing tone,' which the impartial hearer could not make out. The single rider is a raw-boned male figure, 'with lank hair reaching below his cheeks,' hat drawn close over his brows, 'nose rising slightly in the middle,' of abstruse 'down look,' and large dangerous jaws strictly closed; he sings not, sits there covered, and is sung to by the others bare. Amid pouring deluges and mud knee-deep, 'so that the rain ran in at their necks and vented it at their hose and breeches'; a spectacle to the west of England and posterity! singing as above; answering no question except in song. From Bedminster to Ratcliffgate, along the streets to the High Cross of Bristol; at the High Cross they are laid hold of by the authorities; turn out to be James Nayler and Company."

Truly, a more pitiful example of "hero-worship," is not well to be conceived of. Instead of taking the rational view of it, however, and mercifully shutting up the actors in a mad-house, the authorities of that day, conceiving it to be a stupendous blasphemy, and themselves God's avengers in the matter, sent Nayler, under strong guard, up to London, to be examined before the Parliament. After long and tedious examinations and cross-questionings, and still more tedious debates, some portion of which, not uninstructive to the reader, may still be found in "Burton's Diary," the following horrible resolution was agreed upon :

> That James Nayler be set in the pillory, with his head in the pillory in the Palace Yard, Westminster, during the space of two hours on Thursday next; and be whipped by the hangman through the streets from Westminster to the Old Exchange, and there, likewise, be set in the pillory, with his head in the pillory for the space of two hours, between eleven and one, on Saturday next, in each place wearing a paper containing a description of his crimes; and that at the Old Exchange his tongue be bored through with a hot iron, and that he be there stigmatized on the forehead with the letter "B", and that he be afterward sent to Bristol, to be conveyed into and through the said city on horseback with his face backward, and there, also, publicly whipped the next market day after he comes thither; that from thence he be committed to prison in Bridewell, London, and there restrained from the society of all people, and there to labor hard until he shall be released by Parliament; and during that time be debarred the use of pen, ink, and paper; and have no relief except what he earns by his daily labor.

Such, neither more nor less, was, in the opinion of Parliament, required on their part to appease the Divine vengeance. The sentence was pronounced on the 17th of the Twelfth Month; the entire time of the Parliament for the two months previous having been occupied with the case. The Presbyterians in that body were ready enough to make the most of an offense committed by one who had been an Independent; the Independents, to escape the stigma of extenuating the crimes of one of their quondam brethren, vied with their antagonists in shrieking over the atrocity of Nayler's blasphemy, and in urging its severe punishment. Here and there, among both classes, were men disposed to leniency; and more than one earnest plea was made for merciful dealing with a man whose reason was evidently unsettled, and who was, therefore, a fitting object of compassion; whose crime, if it could indeed be called one, was evidently the result of a clouded intellect, and not of willful intention of evil. On the other hand, many were in favor of putting him to death as a sort of peace-offering to the clergy, who, as a matter of course, were greatly scandalized by Nayler's blasphemy, and still more by the refusal of his sect to pay tithes, or recognize their divine commission.

Nayler was called into the Parliament House to receive his sentence. "I do not know mine offense," he said mildly. "You shall know it," said Sir Thomas Widrington, "by your sentence." When the sentence was read, he attempted to speak, but was silenced. "I pray God," said Nayler, "that he may not lay this to your charge."

The next day, the 18th of the Twelfth Month, he stood in the pillory two hours, in the chill winter air, and was then stripped and scourged by the hangman, at the tail of a cart, through the streets. Three hundred and ten stripes were inflicted; his back and arms were horribly cut and mangled, and his feet crushed and bruised by the feet of horses treading on him in the crowd. He bore all with uncomplaining patience; but was so far exhausted by his sufferings, that it was found necessary to postpone the execution of the residue of the sentence for one week. The terrible severity of his sentence, and his meek endurance of it, had, in the mean time, powerfully affected many of the humane and generous of all classes in the city; and a petition for the remission of the remaining part of the penalty was numerously signed and presented to Parliament. A debate ensued upon it, but its prayer was rejected. Application was then made to Cromwell, who addressed a letter to the speaker of the house, inquiring into the affair, protesting an "abhorrence and detestation of giving or occasioning the least countenance to such opinions and practices" as were imputed to Nayler; "yet, we being intrusted in the present government on behalf of the people of these nations, and not knowing how far such proceeding, entered into wholly without us, may extend in the consequence of it, do hereby desire the house may let us know the grounds and reasons whereon they have proceeded." From this, it is not unlikely that the Protector might have been disposed to clemency, and to look with a degree of charity upon the weakness and errors of one of his old and tried soldiers who had striven like a brave man, as he was, for the rights and liberties of Englishmen; but the clergy here interposed, and vehemently, in the name of God and His Church, demanded that the executioner should finish his work. Five of the most eminent of them, names well known in the Protectorate, Caryl, Manton, Nye, Griffith, and Reynolds, were deputed by Parliament to visit the mangled prisoner. A reasonable request was made, that some impartial person might be present, that justice might be done Nayler in the report of his answers. This was refused. It was, however, agreed that the conversation should be written down and a copy of it left with the jailer. He was asked if he was sorry for his blasphemies. He said he did not know to what blasphemies they alluded; that he did believe in Jesus Christ; that He had taken up His dwelling in his own heart, and for the testimony of Him he now suffered. "I believe," said one of the ministers, "in a Christ who was never in any man's heart." "I know no such Christ," rejoined the prisoner; "the Christ I witness to, fills Heaven and Earth, and dwells in the hearts of all true believers." On being asked why he allowed the women to adore and worship him, he said, he "denied bowing to the creature; but if they beheld the power of Christ, wherever it was, and bowed to it, he could not resist it, or say aught against it."

After some further parley, the reverend visitors grew angry, threw the written record of the conversation in the fire, and left the prison to report the prisoner incorrigible.

On the 27th of the month, he was again led out of his cell and placed upon the pillory. Thousands of citizens were gathered around, many of them earnestly protesting against the extreme cruelty of his punishment. Robert Rich, an influential and honorable merchant, followed him up to the pillory, with expressions of great sympathy, and held him by the hand while the red-hot iron was pressed through his tongue and the brand was placed on his forehead. He was next sent to Bristol, and publicly whipped through the principal streets of that city; and again brought back to the Bridewell prison, where he remained about two years, shut out from all intercourse with his fellow-beings. At the expiration of this period, he was released by order of Parliament. In the solitude of his cell, he said the angel of patience had been with him. Through the cloud which had so long rested over him, the clear light of truth shone in upon his spirit; the weltering chaos of a disordered intellect settled into the calm peace of a reconciliation with God and man. His first act on leaving prison was to visit Bristol, the scene of his melancholy fall. There he publicly confessed his errors, in the eloquent earnestness of a contrite spirit, humbled in view of the past, yet full of thanksgiving and praise for the great boon of forgiveness. A writer who was present says, the "assembly was tendered, and broken into tears; there were few dry eyes, and many were bowed in their minds."

In a paper, which he published soon after, he acknowledges his lamentable delusion. "Condemned for ever," he said, "be all those false worships with which any have idolized my person in that Night of my Temptation, when the Power of Darkness was above me; all that did in any way tend to dishonor the Lord, or draw the minds of any from the measure of Christ Jesus in themselves, to look at flesh, which is as grass; or to ascribe that to the visible which belongs to Him." "Darkness came over me through want of watchfulness and obedience to the pure Eye of God. I was taken captive from the true light; I was walking in the night, as a wandering bird fit for a prey. And if the Lord of all my mercies had not rescued me, I had perished; for I was as one appointed to death and destruction, and there was none to deliver me." "It is in my heart to confess to God, and before men, my folly and offense in that day; yet there were many things formed against me in that day, to take away my life, and bring scandal upon the truth, of which I was not guilty at all." "The provocation of that Time of Temptation was exceeding great against the Lord; yet He left me not; for when Darkness was above, and the Adversary so prevailed, that all things were turned and perverted against my right seeing, hearing, or understanding; only a secret hope and faith I had in my God, whom I had served, that He would bring me through it, and to the end of it, and that I should again see the day of my redemption from under it all; this quieted my soul in its greatest tribulation." He concludes his confession with these words: "He who hath saved my soul from death, who hath lifted my feet up out of the pit, even to Him be glory forever; and let every troubled soul trust in Him, for his mercy endureth forever!"

Among his papers, written soon after his release, is a remarkable prayer, or rather thanksgiving. The limit I have prescribed to myself will only allow me to copy an extract:

It is in my heart to praise Thee, O my God! let me never forget Thee, what Thou hast been to me in the night, by Thy presence in my hour of trial, when I was beset in darkness; when I was cast out as a wandering bird; when I was assaulted with strong temptations, then Thy presence, in secret, did preserve me; and in a low state I felt Thee near me; when my way was through the sea, when I passed under the mountains, there wast Thou present with me; when the weight of the hills was upon me, Thou upheldest me; Thou didst fight on my part when I wrestled with death; when darkness would have shut me up, Thy light shone about me; when my work was in the furnace, and I passed through the fire, by Thee I was not consumed. When I beheld the dreadful visions, and was among the fiery spirits, Thy faith staid me, else through fear I had fallen. I saw Thee, and believed, so that the enemy could not prevail.

After speaking of his humiliation and sufferings, which Divine Mercy had overruled for his spiritual good, he thus concludes:

Thou didst lift me out from the pit, and set me forth in the sight of my enemies; Thou proclaimedst liberty to the captive; Thou calledst my acquaintances near me; they to whom I had been a wonder looked upon me; and in Thy love I obtained favor with those who had deserted me. Then did gladness swallow up sorrow, and I forsook my troubles; and I said, How good is it that man be proved in the night, that he may know his folly; that every mouth may become silent, until Thou makest man known unto himself, and hath slain the boaster, and shown him the vanity which vexeth Thy spirit.

All honor to the Quakers of that day, that at the risk of misrepresentation and calumny they received back to their communion their greatly erring, but deeply repentant, brother. His life, ever after, was one of self-denial and jealous watchfulness over himself—blameless and beautiful in its humility and lowly charity.

Thomas Ellwood, in his autobiography for the year 1659, mentions Nayler, whom he met in company with Edward Burrough at the house of Milton's friend, Pennington. Ellwood's father held a discourse with the two Quakers on their doctrine of free and universal grace. "*James Nailer*," says Ellwood, "handled the subject with so much perspicuity and clear demonstration, that his reasoning seemed to be irresistible. As for Edward Burrough, he was a brisk young Man, of a ready Tongue, and might have been for aught I then knew a Scholar, which made me less admire his Way of Reasoning. But what dropt from *James Nailer* had the greater Force upon me, because he lookt like a simple Countryman, having the appearance of a Husbandman or Shepherd."

In the latter part of the Eighth Month, 1660, he left London, on foot, to visit his wife and children in Wakefield. As he journeyed on, the sense of a solemn change about to take place seemed with him; the shadow of the eternal world fell over him. As he passed through Huntingdon, a friend who saw him describes him as "in an awful and weighty frame of mind, as if he had been redeemed from earth, and a stranger on it, seeking a better home and inheritance." A few miles beyond the town he was found, in the dusk of the evening, very ill, and was taken to the house of a friend, who lived not far distant. He died shortly after, expressing his gratitude for the kindness of his attendants, and invoking blessings upon them. About two hours before his death he spoke to the friend at his bedside these remarkable words, solemn as eternity, and beautiful as the love which fills it:

> There is a spirit which I feel which delights to do no evil, nor to avenge any wrong; but delights to endure all things, in hope to enjoy its own in the end; its hope is to outlive all wrath and contention, and to weary out all exultation and cruelty, or whatever is of a nature contrary to itself. It sees to the end of all temptations; as it bears no evil in itself, so it conceives none in thought to any other; if it be betrayed, it bears it, for its ground and spring is the mercy and forgiveness of God. Its crown is meekness; its life is everlasting love unfeigned; it takes its kingdom with entreaty, and not with contention, and keeps it by lowliness of mind. In God alone it can rejoice, though none else regard it, or can own its life. It is conceived in sorrow, and brought forth with none to pity it; nor doth it murmur at grief and oppression. It never rejoiceth but through sufferings, for with the world's joy it is murdered. I found it alone, being forsaken. I have fellowship therein with them who lived in dens and desolate places of the earth, who through death obtained resurrection and eternal Holy Life.

So died James Nayler. He was buried in "Thomas Parnell's burying-ground, at King's Rippon," in a green nook of rural England. Wrong and violence, and temptation and sorrow and evil-speaking could reach him no more. And in taking leave of him, let us say with old Joseph Wyeth, where he touches upon this case in his *Anguis Flagellatus:* "Let none insult, but take heed lest they also, in the hour of *their* temptation, do fall away."

ANDREW MARVELL.

They who with a good conscience and an upright heart do their civil duties in the sight of God, and in their several places, to resist tyranny and the violence of superstition banded both against them, will never seek to be forgiven that which may justly be attributed to their immortal praise.—*Answer to Eikon Basilike.*

AMONG the great names which adorned the Protectorate,—that period of intense mental activity, when political and religious rights and duties were thoroughly discussed by strong and earnest statesmen and theologians,—that of Andrew Marvell, the friend of Milton, and Latin Secretary of Cromwell, deserves honorable mention. The magnificent prose of Milton, long neglected, is now perhaps as frequently read as his great epic; but the writings of his friend and fellow secretary, devoted like his own to the cause of freedom and the rights of the peoble, are scarcely known to the present generation. It is true that Marvell's political pamphlets were less elaborate and profound than those of the author of the glorious Defense of Unlicensed Printing. He was light, playful, witty, and sarcastic; he lacked the stern dignity, the terrible invective, the bitter scorn, the crushing, annihilating retort, the grand and solemn eloquence, and the devout appeals, which render immortal the controversial works of Milton. But he, too, has left his footprints on his age; he, too, has written for posterity that which they "will not willingly let die." As one of the inflexible defenders of English liberty, sowers of the seed, the fruits of which we are now reaping, he has a higher claim on the kind regards of this generation than his merits as a poet, by no means inconsiderable, would warrant.

Andrew Marvell was born in Kingston-upon-Hull, in 1620. At the age of eighteen he entered Trinity College, whence he was enticed by the Jesuits, then actively seeking proselytes. After remaining with them a short time, his father found him, and brought him back to his studies. On leaving college, he traveled on the Continent. At Rome he wrote his first satire, a humorous critique upon Richard Flecknoe, an English Jesuit and verse writer, whose lines, on Silence, Charles Lamb quotes in one of his Essays. It is supposed that he made his first acquaintance with Milton in Italy.

At Paris he made the Abbot de Manihan the subject of another satire. The abbot pretended to skill in the arts of magic, and used to prognosticate the fortunes of people from the character of their handwriting. At what period he returned from his travels, we are not aware. It is stated, by some of his biographers, that he was sent as secretary of a Turkish mission. In 1653, he was appointed the tutor of Cromwell's nephew; and four years after, doubtless through the instrumentality of his friend

Milton, he received the honorable appointment of Latin Secretary of the Commonwealth. In 1658 he was selected by his townsmen of Hull to represent them in Parliament. In this service he continued until 1663, when, notwithstanding his sturdy republican principles, he was appointed secretary to the Russian embassy. On his return, in 1665, he was again elected to Parliament, and continued in the public service until the prorogation of the Parliament of 1675.

The boldness, the uncompromising integrity, and irreproachable consistency of Marvell, as a statesman, have secured for him the honorable appellation of "the British Aristides." Unlike too many of his old associates under the Protectorate, he did not change with the times. He was a republican in Cromwell's day, and neither threats of assassination, nor flatteries, nor proffered bribes, could make him anything else in that of Charles II. He advocated the rights of the people, at a time when patriotism was regarded as ridiculous folly; when a general corruption, spreading downward from a lewd and abominable court, had made legislation a mere scramble for place and emolument. English history presents no period so disgraceful as the Restoration. To use the words of Macaulay, it was "a day of servitude without loyalty, and sensuality without love; of dwarfish talents and gigantic vices, the paradise of cold hearts and narrow minds; the golden age of the coward, the bigot, and the slave. The principles of liberty were the scoff of every grinning courtier, and the Anathema Maranatha of every fawning dean." It is the peculiar merit of Milton and Marvell that in such an age they held fast their integrity, standing up in glorious contrast with the clerical apostates and traitors to the cause of England's liberty.

In the discharge of his duties as a statesman, Marvell was as punctual and conscientious as our own venerable Apostle of Freedom, John Quincy Adams. He corresponded every post with his constituents, keeping them fully apprised of all that transpired at court or in Parliament. He spoke but seldom, but his great personal influence was exerted privately upon the members of the Commons as well as upon the Peers. His wit, accomplished manners, and literary eminence made him a favorite at the court itself. The voluptuous and careless monarch laughed over the biting satire of the republican poet, and heartily enjoyed his lively conversation. It is said that numerous advances were made to him by the courtiers of Charles II, but he was found to be incorruptible. The personal compliments of the King, the encomiums of Rochester, the smiles and flatteries of the frail but fair and high-born ladies of the Court ; nay, even the golden offers of the King's treasurer, who, climbing with difficulty to his obscure retreat on an upper floor of a court in the Strand, laid a tempting bribe of £1000 before him, on the very day when he had been compelled to borrow a guinea, were all lost upon the inflexible patriot. He stood up manfully, in an age of persecution, for religious liberty; opposed the oppressive *excise*, and demanded frequent Parliaments and a fair representation of the people.

In 1672, Marvell engaged in a controversy with the famous high churchman, Dr. Parker, who had taken the lead in urging the persecution of nonconformists. In one of the works of this arrogant divine he says that "it is absolutely necessary to the peace and government of the world, that the supreme magistrate should be vested with power to govern and conduct the consciences of subjects in affairs of religion. Princes may, with less hazard, give liberty to men's vices and debaucheries, than to their consciences." And, speaking of the various sects of nonconformists, he counsels princes and legislators that "tenderness and indulgence to such men is to nourish vipers in their own bowels, and the most sottish neglect of our quiet and security." Marvell replied to him in a severely satirical pamphlet, which provoked a reply from the Doctor. Marvell rejoined with a rare combination of wit and argument. The effect of his sarcasm on the Doctor and his supporters may be inferred from an anonymous note sent him, in which the writer threatens by the eternal God to cut his throat, if he uttered any more libels upon Dr. Parker. Bishop Burnet remarks that "Marvell writ in a burlesque strain, but with so peculiar and so entertaining a conduct that from the King down to the tradesman his books were read with great pleasure, and not only humbled Parker, but his whole party, for Marvell had all the wits on his side." The Bishop further remarks that Marvell's satire "gave occasion to the only piece of modesty with which Dr. Parker was ever charged, viz.: of withdrawing from town, and not importuning the press for some years, since even a face of brass must grow red when it is burnt as his has been." Dean Swift, in commenting upon the usual fate of controversial pamphlets, which seldom live beyond their generation, says: "There is indeed an exception, when a great genius undertakes to expose a foolish piece; so we still read Marvell's answer to Parker with pleasure, though the book it answers be sunk long ago."

Perhaps, in the entire compass of our language, there is not to be found a finer piece of satirical writing than Marvell's famous parody of the speeches of Charles II, in which the private vices and public inconsistencies of the King, and his gross violations of his pledges on coming to the throne, are exposed with the keenest wit and the most laugh-provoking irony. Charles, himself, although doubtless annoyed by it, could not refrain from joining in the mirth which it excited at his expense.

The friendship between Marvell and Milton remained firm and unbroken to the last. The former exerted himself to save his illustrious friend from persecution, and omitted no opportunity to defend him as a politician and to eulogize him as a poet. In 1654, he presented to Cromwell Milton's noble tract in Defense of the People of England, and, in writing to the author, says of the work, "When I consider how equally it teems and rises with so many figures, it seems to me a Trajan's column, in whose winding ascent we see embossed the several monuments of your learned victories." He was one of the first to appreciate Paradise Lost, and to commend it in some admirable lines. One couplet is exceedingly beautiful, in its reference to the author's blindness:

> Just Heaven, thee like Tiresias to requite,
> Rewards with prophecy thy loss of sight.

His poems, written in the "snatched leisure" of an active political life, bear marks of haste, and are very unequal. In the midst of passages of pastoral description worthy of Milton himself, feeble lines and hackneyed phrases occur. His "Nymph lamenting the Death of her Fawn" is a finished and elaborate piece, full of grace and tenderness. "Thoughts in a Garden" will be remembered by the quotations of that exquisite critic, Charles Lamb. How pleasant is this picture!

> What wondrous life is this I lead!
> Ripe apples drop about my head,
> The luscious clusters of the vine
> Upon my mouth do crush their wine;
> The nectarine and curious peach
> Into my hands themselves do reach;
> Stumbling on melons as I pass,
> Ensnared with flowers, I fall on grass.
>
> Here at this fountain's sliding foot,
> Or at the fruit tree's mossy root,

Casting the body's vest aside,
My soul into the boughs does glide.

There like a bird it sits and sings,
And whets and claps its silver wings;
And, till prepared for longer flight,
Waves in its plumes the various light.

How well the skillful gard'ner drew
Of flowers and herbs this dial true!
Where, from above, the milder sun
Does through a fragrant zodiac run;
And, as it works, the industrious bee
Computes his time as well as we.
How could such sweet and wholesome hours
Be reckoned but with herbs and flowers!"

One of his longer poems, "Appleton House," contains passages of admirable description, and many not unpleasing conceits. Witness the following:

Thus I, an easy philosopher,
Among the birds and trees confer,
And little now to make me wants,
Or of the fowl or of the plants.
Give me but wings, as they, and I
Straight floating on the air shall fly;
Or turn me but, and you shall see
I am but an inverted tree.
Already I begin to call
In their most learned original;
And, where I language want, my signs
The bird upon the bough divines.
No leaf does tremble in the wind,
Which I returning cannot find.
Out of these scattered Sybil's leaves,
Strange prophecies my fancy weaves;

What Rome, Greece, Palestine, e'er said,
I in this light Mosaic read.
Under this antic cope I move,
Like some great prelate of the grove;
Then, languishing at ease, I toss
On pallets thick with velvet moss;
While the wind, cooling through the boughs,
Flatters with air my panting brows.
Thanks for my rest, ye mossy banks!
And unto you, cool zephyrs, thanks!
Who, as my hair, my thoughts too shed,
And winnow from the chaff my head.
How safe, methinks, and strong behind
These trees have I encamped my mind!

Here is a picture of a piscatorial idler and his trout stream, worthy of the pencil of Izaak Walton:

See in what wanton harmless folds
It everywhere the meadow holds:
Where all things gaze themselves, and doubt
If they be in it or without;
And for this shade, which therein shines,
Narcissus-like, the sun too pines.
Oh! what a pleasure 'tis to hedge
My temples here in heavy sedge;
Abandoning my lazy side,
Stretched as a bank unto the tide;
Or, to suspend my sliding foot
On the osier's undermining root,
And in its branches tough to hang,
While at my lines the fishes twang.

A little poem of Marvell's, which he calls "Eyes and Tears," has the following passages:

How wisely Nature did agree
With the same eyes to weep and see!
That, having viewed the object vain,
They might be ready to complain.
And, since the self-deluding sight
In a false angle takes each height,
These tears, which better measure all,
Like watery lines and plummets fall.

Happy are they whom grief doth bless,
That weep the more, and see the less;
And, to preserve their sight more true,
Bathe still their eyes in their own dew;
So Magdalen, in tears more wise,
Dissolved those captivating eyes,
Whose liquid chains could, flowing, meet
To fetter her Redeemer's feet.
The sparkling glance, that shoots desire,
Drenched in those tears, does lose its fire;
Yea, oft the Thunderer pity takes,
And there His hissing lightning slakes.
The incense is to Heaven dear,
Not as a perfume, but a tear;
And stars shine lovely in the night,
But as they seem the tears of light.
Ope, then, mine eyes, your double sluice,
And practice so your noblest use;
For others, too, can see or sleep,
But only human eyes can weep.

The "Bermuda Emigrants" has some happy lines, as the following:

He hangs in shade the orange bright,
Like golden lamps in a green night.

Or this, which doubtless suggested a couplet in Moore's Canadian Boat Song:

> And all the way, to guide the chime,
> With falling oars they kept the time.

His facetious and burlesque poetry was much admired in his day; but a great portion of it referred to persons and events no longer of general interest. The satire on Holland is an exception. There is nothing in its way superior to it in our language. Many of his best pieces were originally written in Latin, and afterward translated by himself. There is a splendid Ode to Cromwell,—a worthy companion of Milton's glorious sonnet,—which is not generally known, and which we transfer entire to our pages. Its simple dignity, and the melodious flow of its versification, commend themselves more to our feelings than its eulogy of war. It is energetic and impassioned, and probably affords a better idea of the author, as an actor in the stirring drama of his time, than the "soft Lydian airs" of the poems that we have quoted:

AN HORATIAN ODE UPON CROMWELL'S RETURN FROM IRELAND.

> The forward youth that would appear
> Must now forsake his Muses dear;
> Nor in the shadows sing
> His numbers languishing.
>
> 'Tis time to leave the books in dust,
> And oil the unused armor's rust;

Removing from the wall
The corslet of the hall.

So restless Cromwell could not cease
In the inglorious arts of peace,
But through adventurous war
Urged his active star;

And, like the three-fork'd lightning, first
Breaking the clouds wherein it nurst,
Did thorough his own side
His fiery way divide.

For 'tis all one to courage high,
The emulous, or enemy;
And with such to inclose
Is more than to oppose.

Then burning through the air he went,
And palaces and temples rent;
And Cæsar's head at last
Did through his laurels blast.

'Tis madness to resist or blame
The face of angry Heaven's flame;
And, if we would speak true,
Much to the man is due,

Who, from his private gardens, where
He lived reserved and austere
(As if his highest plot
To plant the bergamot),

Could by industrious valor climb
To ruin the great work of time,
And cast the kingdoms old
Into another mold!

Though justice against fate complain,
And plead the ancient rights in vain—
  But those do hold or break,
  As men are strong or weak.

Nature, that hateth emptiness,
Allows of penetration less,
  And therefore must make room
  Where greater spirits come.

What field of all the civil war,
Where his were not the deepest scar?
  And Hampton shows what part
  He had of wiser art;

Where, twining subtle fears with hope,
He wove a net of such a scope,
  That Charles himself might chase
  To Carisbrook's narrow case:

That hence the royal actor borne,
The tragic scaffold might adorn;
  While round the armed bands
  Did clap their bloody hands.

He nothing common did or mean
Upon that memorable scene,
  But with his keener eye
  The ax's edge did try:

Nor called the gods, with vulgar spite,
To vindicate his helpless right!
  But bowed his comely head,
  Down, as upon a bed.

This was that memorable hour,
Which first assured the forced power;
  So when they did design
  The Capitol's first line,

A bleeding head, where they begun,
Did fright the architects to run;
  And yet in that the state
  Foresaw its happy fate.

And now the Irish are ashamed
To see themselves in one year tamed;
  So much one man can do,
  That does best act and know.

They can affirm his praises best,
And have, though overcome, confest
  How good he is, how just,
  And fit for highest trust.

Nor yet grown stiffer by command,
But still in the Republic's hand,
  How fit he is to sway
  That can so well obey.

He to the Commons' feet presents
A kingdom for his first year's rents,
  And, what he may, forbears
  His fame to make it theirs,

And has his sword and spoils ungirt,
To lay them at the public's skirt;
  So when the falcon high
  Falls heavy from the sky,

She, having killed, no more does search,
But on the next green bough to perch,
  Where, when he first does lure,
  The falconer has her sure.

What may not, then, our isle presume,
While Victory his crest does plume?
  What may not others fear,
  If thus he crowns each year?

As Cæsar, he, ere long, to Gaul;
To Italy as Hannibal,
  And to all States not free
  Shall climacteric be.

The Pict no shelter now shall find
Within his parti-contour'd mind;
  But from his valor sad
  Shrink underneath the plaid,

Happy if in the tufted break
The English hunter him mistake,
  Nor lay his hands a near
  The Caledonian deer.

But thou, the war's and fortune's son,
March indefatigably on;
  And, for the last effect,
  Still keep the sword erect.

Besides the force, it has to fright
The spirits of the shady night:
  The same arts that did gain
  A power, must it maintain.

Marvell was never married. The modern critic, who affirms that bachelors have done the most to exalt woman into a divinity, might have quoted his extravagant panegyric of Maria Fairfax as an apt illustration:

'Tis she that to these gardens gave
The wondrous beauty which they have;
She straitness on the woods bestows,
To her the meadow sweetness owes,
Nothing could make the river be
So crystal pure but only she—

She, yet more pure, sweet, strait, and fair,
Than gardens, woods, meads, rivers are!
Therefore, what first she on them spent
They gratefully again present
The meadow carpets where to tread,
The garden flowers to crown her head;
And for a glass the limpid brook,
Where she may all her beauties look;
But, since she would not have them seen,
The wood about her draws a screen;
For she, to higher beauty raised,
Disdains to be for lesser praised;
She counts her beauty to converse
In all the languages as hers,
Nor yet in those herself employs.
But for the wisdom, not the noise;
Nor yet that wisdom could affect,
But as 'tis Heaven's dialect.

It has been the fashion of a class of shallow Church and State defenders to ridicule the great men of the Commonwealth, the sturdy republicans of England, as sour-featured, hard-hearted ascetics, enemies of the fine arts and polite literature. The works of Milton and Marvell, the prose poem of Harrington, and the admirable discourses of Algernon Sydney, are a sufficient answer to this accusation. To none has it less application than to the subject of our sketch. He was a genial, warm-hearted man, an elegant scholar, a finished gentleman at home, and the life of every circle which he entered, whether that of the gay court of Charles II, amid such men as Rochester and L'Estrange, or that of the republican philosophers who assembled at Miles's

Coffee House, where he discussed plans of a free representative government with the author of "Oceana," and Cyriack Skinner, that friend of Milton, whom the bard has immortalized in the sonnet which so pathetically, yet heroically, alludes to his own blindness. Men of all parties enjoyed his wit and graceful conversation. His personal appearance was altogether in his favor. A clear, dark, Spanish complexion; long hair of jetty blackness, falling in graceful wreaths to his shoulders; dark eyes, full of expression and fire; a finely chiseled chin, and a mouth whose soft voluptuousness scarcely gave token of the steady purpose and firm will of the inflexible statesman; these, added to the *prestige* of his genius, and the respect which a lofty, self-sacrificing patriotism extorts even from those who would fain corrupt and bribe it, gave him a ready passport to the fashionable society of the metropolis. He was one of the few who mingled in that society, and escaped its contamination, and who,

> Amidst the wavering days of sin,
> Kept himself icy chaste and pure.

The tone and temper of his mind may be most fitly expressed in his own paraphrase of Horace:

> Climb at Court for me that will,
> Tottering Favor's pinnacle;
> All I seek is to lie still!
> Settled in some secret nest,
> In calm leisure let me rest;
> And, far off the public stage,
> Pass away my silent age.

Thus, when, without noise, unknown,
  I have lived out all my span,
I shall die without a groan,
  An old, honest countryman.
Who, exposed to other's eyes,
Into his own heart ne'er pries,
Death's to him a strange surprise.

He died suddenly, in 1678, while in attendance at a popular meeting of his old constituents at Hull. His health had previously been remarkably good; and it was supposed by many that he was poisoned by some of his political or clerical enemies. His monument, erected by his grateful constituency, bears the following inscription:

Near this place lyeth the body of Andrew Marvell, Esq., a man so endowed by Nature, so improved by Education, Study, and Travel, so consummated by Experience, that, joining the peculiar graces of Wit and Learning, with a singular penetration and strength of judgment; and exercising all these in the whole course of his life, with an unutterable steadiness in the ways of Virtue, he became the ornament and example of his age, beloved by good men, feared by bad, admired by all, though imitated by few; and scarce paralleled by any. But a Tombstone can neither contain his character, nor is Marble necessary to transmit it to posterity; it is engraved in the minds of this generation, and will be always legible in his inimitable writings, nevertheless. He having served twenty years successively in Parliament, and that with such Wisdom, Dexterity, and Courage as becomes a true Patriot, the town of Kingston-upon-Hull, from whence he was deputed to that Assembly, lamenting in his death the public loss, have erected this Monument of their Grief and their Gratitude, 1688.

Thus lived and died Andrew Marvell. His memory is the inheritance of Americans as well as Englishmen. His example commends itself in an especial manner to the legislators of our Republic. Integrity and fidelity to principle are as greatly needed at this time in our Halls of Congress as in the Parliaments of the Restoration; men are required who can feel, with Milton, that "it is high honor done them from God, and a special mark of His favor, to have been selected to stand upright and steadfast in His cause, dignified with the defense of Truth and public liberty."

JOHN ROBERTS.

THOMAS CARLYLE, in his history of the stout and sagacious Monk of St. Edmunds, has given us a fine picture of the actual life of Englishmen in the middle centuries. The dim cell-lamp of the somewhat apocryphal Jocelin of Brakelond, becomes in his hands a huge Drummond light, shining over the dark ages like the naphtha-fed cressets over Pandemonium, proving, as he says in his own quaint way, that "England in the year 1200 was no dreamland, but a green, solid place, which grew corn and several other things; the sun shone on it; the vicissitudes of seasons and human fortunes were there; cloth was woven, ditches dug, furrowed fields plowed, and houses built." And if, as the writer just quoted insists, it is a matter of no small importance to make it credible to the present generation, that the Past is not a confused dream of thrones and battlefields, creeds and constitutions, but a reality, substantial as hearth and home, harvest field and smith shop, merry-making and death, could make it, we shall not wholly waste our own time and that of our readers, in inviting them to look with us at the rural life of England two centuries ago, through the eyes of John Roberts and his worthy son Daniel, yeomen, of Siddington, near Cirencester.

The "Memoirs of John Roberts, alias Haywood, by his son, Daniel Roberts" (the second edition, printed verbatim from the original one, with its picturesque array of italics and capital letters), is to be found only in a few of our old Quaker libraries. It opens with some account of the family. The father of the elder Roberts "lived reputably, on a little estate of his own," and it is mentioned as noteworthy that he married a sister of a gentleman in the Commission of the Peace. Coming of age about the beginning of the civil wars, John and one of his young neighbors enlisted in the service of Parliament. Hearing that Cirencester had been taken by the King's forces, they obtained leave of absence to visit their friends, for whose safety they naturally felt solicitous. The following account of the reception they met with from the drunken and ferocious troopers of Charles I, the "bravos of Alsatia and the pages of Whitehall," throws a ghastly light upon the horrors of civil war:

"As they were passing by Cirencester, they were discovered and pursued by two soldiers of the King's party, then in possession of the town. Seeing themselves pursued, they quitted their horses, and took to their heels; but, by reason of their accoutrements, could make little speed. They came up with my father first; and, though he begged for quarter, none they would give him, but laid on him with their swords, cutting and slashing his hands and arms, which he held up to save his head; as the marks upon them did long after testify. At length it pleased the Almighty to put it into his mind to fall down on his face; which he did. Hereupon the soldiers, being on horseback, cried to each other, *Alight, and cut his throat!* but neither of them did; yet continued to strike and prick him about the jaws, till they thought him dead. Then they left him, and pursued his neighbor, whom they presently overtook and killed. Soon after they had left my father, it was said in his heart, *Rise, and flee for thy life!* Which call he obeyed; and, starting upon his feet, his enemies espied him in motion, and pursued him again. He ran down a steep hill, and through a river which ran at the bottom of it; though with exceeding difficulty, his boots filling with water, and his wounds bleeding very much. They followed him to the top of the hill; but seeing he had got over, pursued him no farther."

The surgeon who attended him was a Royalist, and bluntly told his bleeding patient that if he had met him in the street he would have killed him himself, but now he was willing to cure him. On his recovery, young Roberts again entered the army, and continued in it until the overthrow of the Monarchy. On his return, he married "Lydia Tindall, of the denomination of *Puritans*." A majestic figure rises before us, on reading the statement that Sir Matthew Hale, afterward Lord Chief Justice of England, the irreproachable Jurist and Judicial Saint, was "his wife's kinsman, and drew her marriage settlement."

No stronger testimony to the high-toned morality and austere virtue of the Puritan yeomanry of England can be adduced than the fact, that of the fifty thousand soldiers who were discharged on the accession of Charles II, and left to shift for themselves, comparatively few, if any, became chargeable to their parishes, although at that very time one out of six of the English population were unable to support themselves. They carried into their farm-fields and workshops the strict habits of Cromwell's discipline; and, in toiling to repair their wasted fortunes, they manifested the same heroic fortitude and self-denial which in war had made them such formidable and efficient "Soldiers of the Lord." With few exceptions, they remained steadfast in their uncompromising nonconformity, abhorring Prelacy and Popery, and entertaining no very orthodox notions with respect to the divine right of kings. From them the Quakers drew their most zealous champions; men who, in renouncing the "carnal weapons" of their old service, found employment for habitual combativeness in hot and wordy sectarian warfare. To this day, the vocabulary of Quakerism abounds in the military phrases and figures which were in use in the Commonwealth's time. Their old force and significance are now in a great measure lost; but one can well imagine that, in the assemblies of the primitive Quakers, such stirring battle-cries and warlike tropes, even when employed in enforcing or illustrating the doctrines of peace, must have made many a stout heart to beat quicker, under its drab coloring, with recollections of Naseby and Preston; transporting many a listener from the benches of his place of worship to the ranks of Ireton and Lambert, and causing him to hear, in the place of the solemn and nasal tones of the preacher, the blast of Rupert's bugles and the answering shout of Cromwell's pikemen: "Let God arise, and let his enemies be scattered!"

Of this class was John Roberts. He threw off his knapsack, and went back to his small homestead, contented with the privilege of supporting himself and family by daily toil, and grumbling, in concert with his old campaign brothers, at the new order of things in Church and State. To his apprehension, the Golden Days of England ended with the parade on Blackheath to receive the restored King. He manifested no reverence for Bishops and Lords, for he felt none. For the Presbyterians he had no good will; they had brought in the King, and they denied the liberty of prophesying. John Milton has expressed the feeling of the Independents and Anabaptists toward this latter class, in that famous line in which he defines Presbyter as "old priest writ large." Roberts was by no means a gloomy fanatic; he had a great deal of shrewdness and humor; loved a quiet joke; and every gambling priest and swearing magistrate in the neighborhood stood in fear of his sharp wit. It was quite in course for such a man to fall in with the Quakers, and he appears to have done so at the first opportunity.

In the year 1665, "it pleased the Lord to send

two women Friends out of the North to Cirencester," who, inquiring after such as feared God, were directed to the house of John Roberts. He received them kindly, and, inviting in some of his neighbors, sat down with them, whereupon, "the Friends spake a few words, which had a good effect." After the meeting was over, he was induced to visit a "Friend" then confined in Banbury jail, whom he found preaching through the grates of his cell to the people in the street. On seeing Roberts, he called to mind the story of Zaccheus, and declared that the word was now to all who were seeking Christ by climbing the tree of knowledge, "Come down, come down; for that which is to be known of God is manifested *within*." Returning home, he went soon after to the parish meeting-house, and, entering with his hat on, the priest noticed him, and stopping short in his discourse, declared that he could not go on while one of the congregation wore his hat. He was thereupon led out of the house, and a rude fellow, stealing up behind, struck him on the back with a heavy stone. "Take that for God's sake," said the ruffian. "So I do," answered Roberts, without looking back to see his assailant, who the next day came and asked his forgiveness for the injury, as he could not sleep in consequence of it.

We next find him attending the Quarter Sessions, where the "Friends" were arraigned for entering Cirencester Church with their hats on. Venturing to utter a word of remonstrance against the sum-mary proceedings of the Court, Justice Stephens demanded his name, and, on being told, exclaimed, in the very tone and temper of Jeffreys, "I've heard of you. I'm glad I have you here. You deserve a stone doublet. There is many an honester man than you hanged." "It may be so," said Roberts, "but what becomes of such as hang honest men?" The Justice snatched a ball of wax, and hurled it at the quiet questioner. "I'll send you to prison," said he; "and if any insurrection or tumult occurs, I'll come and cut your throat with my own sword." A warrant was made out, and he was forthwith sent to the jail. In the evening, Justice Sollis, his uncle, released him, on condition of his promise to appear at the next Sessions. He returned to his home, but in the night following he was impressed with a belief that it was his duty to visit Justice Stephens. Early in the morning, with a heavy heart, without eating or drinking, he mounted his horse and rode toward the residence of his enemy. When he came in sight of the house, he felt strong misgivings that his uncle, Justice Sollis, who had so kindly released him, and his neighbors generally, would condemn him for voluntarily running into danger, and drawing down trouble upon himself and family. He alighted from his horse and sat on the ground in great doubt and sorrow, when a voice seemed to speak within him, "Go, and I will go with thee." The Justice met him at the door. "I am come," said Roberts, "in the fear and dread of Heaven, to warn thee to repent of thy wickedness with speed, lest the Lord send thee to the pit that is bottomless!" This terrible summons awed the Justice; he made Roberts sit down on his couch beside him, declaring that he received the message from God, and asked forgiveness for the wrong he had done him.

The parish vicar of Siddington at this time was George Bull, afterward Bishop of St. David's, whom Macaulay speaks of as the only rural parish priest who, during the latter part of the seventeenth century, was noted as a theologian, or who possessed a respectable library. Roberts refused to pay the vicar his tithes, and the vicar sent him to prison. It was the priest's "Short Method with Dissenters." While the sturdy Nonconformist lay in prison he was visited by the great woman of the neighborhood, Lady Dunch, of Down Amney. "What do you lie in jail for?" inquired the lady. Roberts replied that it was because he could not put bread into the mouth of a hireling priest. The lady suggested that he might let somebody else satisfy the demands of the priest, and that she had a mind to do this herself, as she wished to talk with him on religious subjects. To this Roberts objected; there were poor people who needed her charities, which would be wasted on such devourers as the priests, who, like Pharaoh's lean kine, were eating up the fat and the goodly, without looking a whit the better. But the lady, who seems to have been pleased and amused by the obstinate prisoner, paid the tithe and the jail fees, and set him at liberty, making him fix a day when he would visit her. At the time appointed he went to Down Amney, and was overtaken on the way by the priest of Cirencester, who had been sent for to meet the Quaker. They found the lady ill in bed; but she had them brought to her chamber, being determined not to lose the amusement of hearing a theological discussion, to which she at once urged them, declaring that it would divert her and do her good. The Parson began by accusing the Quakers of holding Popish doctrines. The Quaker retorted by telling him that if he would prove the Quakers like the Papists in one thing, by the help of God he would prove him like them in ten. After a brief and sharp dispute, the priest, finding his adversary's wit too keen for his comfort, hastily took his leave.

The next we hear of Roberts, he is in Gloucester Castle, subjected to the brutal usage of a jailer, who took a malicious satisfaction in thrusting decent and respectable Dissenters, imprisoned for matters of conscience, among felons and thieves. A poor vagabond tinker was hired to play at night on his hautboy and prevent their sleeping; but Roberts spoke to him in such a manner that the instrument fell from his hand; and he told the jailer that he would play no more, though he should hang him up at the door for it.

How he was released from jail does not appear; but the narrative tells us that, some time after, an apparitor came to cite him to the Bishop's Court at Gloucester. When he was brought before the Court,

Bishop Nicholson, a kind-hearted and easy-natured prelate, asked him the number of his children, and how many of them had been *bishoped.*

"None, that I know of," said Roberts.

"What reason," asked the Bishop, "do you give for this?"

"A very good one," said the Quaker; "most of my children were born in Oliver's days, when Bishops were out of fashion."

The Bishop and the Court laughed at this sally, and proceeded to question him touching his views of baptism. Roberts admitted that John had a Divine commission to baptize with water, but that he never heard of anybody else that had. The Bishop reminded him that Christ's disciples baptized. "What's that to me?" responded Roberts. "Paul says he was not sent to baptize, but to preach the Gospel. And if he was not sent, who required it at his hands? Perhaps he had as little thanks for his labor as thou hast for thine; and I would willingly know who sent thee to baptize?"

The Bishop evaded this home question, and told him he was there to answer for not coming to church. Roberts denied the charge; sometimes he went to church, and sometimes it came to him. "I don't call that a church which you do, which is made of wood and stone."

"What do you call it?" asked the Bishop.

"It might be properly called a mass-house," was the reply; "for it was built for that purpose." The Bishop here told him he might go for the present;

he would take another opportunity to convince him of his errors.

The next person called was a Baptist minister, who, seeing that Roberts refused to put off his hat, kept on his also. The Bishop sternly reminded him that he stood before the King's Court, and the representative of the majesty of England; and that, while some regard might be had to the scruples of men who made a conscience of putting off the hat, such contempt could not be tolerated on the part of one who could put it off to every mechanic he met. The Baptist pulled off his hat, and apologized, on the ground of illness.

We find Roberts next following George Fox on a visit to Bristol. On his return, reaching his house late in the evening, he saw a man standing in the moonlight at his door, and knew him to be a bailiff. "Hast thou anything against me?" asked Roberts. "No," said the bailiff, "I've wronged you enough, God forgive me! Those who lie in wait for you are my Lord Bishop's bailiffs; they are merciless rogues. Ever, my master, while you live, please a knave, for an honest man won't hurt you."

The next morning, having, as he thought, been warned by a dream to do so, he went to the Bishop's house at Cleave, near Gloucester. Confronting the Bishop in his own hall, he told him that he had come to know why he was hunting after him with his bailiffs, and why he was his adversary? "The King is your adversary," said the Bishop; "you have broken the King's law." Roberts ventured to deny the justice of the law. "What!" cried the Bishop, "do such men as you find fault with the laws?" "Yes," replied the other stoutly; "and I tell thee plainly to thy face, it is high time wiser men were chosen, to make better laws."

The discourse turning upon the Book of Common Prayer, Roberts asked the Bishop if the sin of idolatry did not consist in worshiping the work of men's hands. The Bishop admitted it, as in the case of Nebuchadnezzar's image.

"Then," said Roberts, "whose hands made your Prayer Book? It could not make itself."

"Do you compare our Prayer Book to Nebuchadnezzar's image?" cried the Bishop.

"Yes," returned Roberts, "that was his image; this is thine. I no more dare bow to thy Common Prayer Book than the Three Children to Nebuchadnezzar's image."

"Yours is a strange upstart religion," said the Bishop.

Roberts told him it was older than his by several hundred years. At this claim of antiquity the Prelate was greatly amused, and told Roberts that if he would make out his case, he should speed the better for it.

"Let me ask thee," said Roberts, "where thy religion was in Oliver's days, when thy Common Prayer Book was as little regarded as an old Almanac; and your priests, with a few honest exceptions, turned with the tide, and if Oliver had put mass in their mouths, would have conformed to it for the sake of their bellies."

"What would you have us do?" asked the Bishop. "Would you have had Oliver cut our throats?"

"No," said Roberts; "but what sort of religion was that which you were afraid to venture your throats for?"

The Bishop interrupted him to say, that in Oliver's days he had never owned any other religion than his own, although he did not dare to openly maintain it as he then did.

"Well," continued Roberts, "if thou didst not think thy religion worth venturing thy throat for then, I desire thee to consider that it is not worth the cutting of other men's throats now for not conforming to it."

"You are right," responded the frank Bishop. "I hope we shall have a care how we cut men's throats."

The following colloquy throws some light on the condition and character of the rural clergy at this period, and goes far to confirm the statements of Macaulay, which many have supposed exaggerated. Baxter's early religious teachers were more exceptionable than even the maudlin mummer whom Roberts speaks of, one of them being "the excellentest stage-player in all the country, and a good gamester and good fellow, who, having received Holy Orders, forged the like for a neighbor's son; who, on the strength of that title, officiated at the desk and altar; and after him came an attorney's clerk, who had tippled himself into so great poverty that he had no other way to live than to preach."

J. ROBERTS. I was bred up under a Common

Prayer Priest; and a poor drunken old Man he was; sometimes he was so drunk he could not say his Prayers, and at best he could but say them; though I think he was by far a better Man than he that is Priest there now.

BISHOP. Who is your Minister now?

J. ROBERTS. My Minister is Christ Jesus, the Minister of the everlasting Covenant; but the present Priest of the Parish is George Bull.

BISHOP. Do you say that drunken old Man was better than Mr. Bull? I tell you, I account Mr. Bull as sound, able, and orthodox a Divine as any we have among us.

J. ROBERTS. I am sorry for that; for if he be one of the best of you, I believe the Lord will not suffer you long. For he is a proud, ambitious, ungodly Man; he hath often sued me at Law, and brought his Servants to swear against me wrongfully. His Servants themselves have confessed to my Servants, that I might have their Ears; for their Master made them drunk, and then told them they were set down in the List as Witnesses against me, and they must swear to it. And so they did, and brought treble Damages. They likewise owned they took Tithes from my Servants, threshed them out, and sold them for their Master. They have also several Times took my Cattle out of my Grounds, drove them to Fairs and Markets, and sold them, without giving me any Account.

BISHOP. I do assure you I will inform Mr. Bull of what you say.

J. ROBERTS. Very well. And if thou pleasest to send for me to face him, I shall make much more appear to his Face than I'll say behind his Back.

After much more discourse, Roberts told the Bishop that if it would do him any good to have him in jail, he would voluntarily go and deliver himself up to the keeper of Gloucester Castle. The good-natured Prelate relented at this, and said he should not be molested or injured, and further manifested his good will by ordering refreshments. One of the Bishop's friends who was present was highly offended by the freedom of Roberts with his Lordship, and undertook to rebuke him, but was so readily answered, that he flew into a rage. "If all the Quakers in England," said he, "are not hanged in a month's time, I'll be hanged for them." "Prithee, friend," quoth Roberts, "remember and be as good as thy word!"

Good old Bishop Nicholson, it would seem, really liked his incorrigible Quaker neighbor, and could enjoy heartily his wit and humor, even when exercised at the expense of his own ecclesiastical dignity. He admired his blunt honesty and courage. Surrounded by flatterers and self-seekers, he found satisfaction in the company and conversation of one who, setting aside all conventionalisms, saw only in my Lord Bishop a poor fellow-probationer, and addressed him on terms of conscious equality. The indulgence which he extended to him, naturally enough provoked many of the inferior clergy, who had been sorely annoyed by the sturdy Dissenter's irreverent witticisms and unsparing ridicule. Vicar Bull, of Siddington, and Priest Careless, of Cirencester, in particular, urged the Bishop to deal sharply with him. The former accused him of dealing in the Black Art, and filled the Bishop's ear with certain marvelous stories of his preternatural sagacity and discernment in discovering cattle which were lost. The Bishop took occasion to inquire into these stories; and was told by Roberts, that, except in a single instance, the discoveries were the result of his acquaintance with the habits of animals, and his knowledge of the localities where they were lost. The circumstance alluded to as an exception, will be best related in his own words:

"I had a poor Neighbor, who had a Wife and six Children, and whom the chief men about us permitted to keep six or seven Cows upon the Waste, which were the principal Support of the Family, and preserved them from becoming chargeable to the Parish. One very stormy night, the Cattle were left in the Yard as usual, but could not be found in the morning. The Man and his Sons had sought them to no purpose; and, after they had been lost four days, his Wife came to me, and, in a great deal of grief, cried, 'O Lord! Master Hayward, we are undone! My Husband and I must go a-begging in our old age! We have lost all our Cows. My Husband and the Boys have been round the country, and can hear nothing of them. I'll down on my bare knees, if you'll stand our Friend!' I desired she would not be in such an agony, and told her she should not down on her knees to me; but I would gladly help them in what I could. 'I know,' said she, 'you are a good Man, and God will hear your Prayers.' I desire thee, said I, to be still and quiet in thy mind; perhaps thy Husband or Sons may hear of them to-day; if not, let thy Husband get a horse, and come to me to-morrow morning as soon as he will; and I think, if it please God, to go with him to seek them. The Woman seemed transported with joy, crying, 'Then we shall have our Cows again.' Her Faith being so strong, brought the great Exercise on me, with strong cries to the Lord that he would be pleased to make me instrumental in his Hand, for the help of the poor Family. In the Morning early comes the old Man. *In the Name of God,* says he, *which Way shall we go to seek them?* I, being deeply concerned in my Mind, did not answer him till he had thrice repeated it; and then I answered, In the Name of God, I would go to seek them; and said (before I was well aware), we will go to Malmsbury, and at the Horse Fair we shall find them. When I had spoken the Words, I was much troubled lest they should not prove true. It was very early, and the first Man we saw, I asked him if he had seen any stray Milch Cows thereabouts? *What manner of Cattle are they?* said he. And the old Man describing their Mark and Number, he told us there were some stood chewing their Cuds in the Horse Fair; but, thinking they belonged to some in the Neighborhood, he did not take particular Notice of them. When we came to the Place, the old Man found them to be his; but suffered his Transports of Joy to rise so high, that I was ashamed of his behavior; for he fell a-hallooing, and threw up his Montier Cap in the Air several times, till he raised the Neighbors out of their Beds to see what was the Matter. 'Oh!' said he, 'I had lost my Cows four or five days ago, and thought I should never see them again; and this honest Neighbor of mine told me this Morning, by his own Fire's Side, nine Miles off, that here I should find them, and here I have them!' Then up goes his Cap again. I begged of the poor Man to be quiet, and take his Cows home, and be thankful; as indeed I was, being reverently bowed in my Spirit before the Lord, in that he was pleased to put the words of Truth into my mouth. And the Man drove his Cattle home, to the great Joy of his Family."

Not long after the interview with the Bishop at his own palace, which has been related, that dignitary, with the Lord Chancellor, in their coaches, and about twenty clergymen on horseback, made a call at the humble dwelling of Roberts, on their way to Tedbury, where the Bishop was to hold a Visitation. "I could not go out of the country without seeing you," said the Prelate, as the farmer came to his coach door and pressed him to alight.

"John," asked Priest Evans, the Bishop's kinsman, "is your house free to entertain such men as we are?"

"Yes, George," said Roberts; "I entertain honest men, and sometimes others."

"My Lord," said Evans, turning to the Bishop, "John's friends are the honest men, and we are the others."

The Bishop told Roberts that they could not then alight, but would gladly drink with him; whereupon, the good wife brought out her best beer. "I commend you, John," quoth the Bishop, as he paused from his hearty draught; "you keep a cup of good beer in your house. I have not drank any that has pleased me better since I left home." The cup passed next to the Chancellor, and finally came to Priest Bull, who thrust it aside, declaring that it was full of hops and heresy. As to Hops, Roberts replied, he could not say; but, as for Heresy, he bade the priest take note, that the Lord Bishop had drank of it, and had found no heresy in the cup.

The Bishop leaned over his coach door and whispered: "John, I advise you to take care you don't offend against the higher Powers. I have heard great complaints against you, that you are the Ringleader of the Quakers in this Country; and that, if you are not suppressed, all will signify nothing. Therefore, pray, John, take care for the future you don't offend any more."

"I like thy Counsel very well," answered Roberts, "and intend to take it. But thou knowest God is the higher Power; and you mortal Men, however advanced in this World, are but the lower Power; and it is only because I endeavor to be obedient to the will of the higher Powers, that the lower Powers are angry with me. But I hope, with the assistance of God, to take thy Counsel, and be subject to the higher Powers, let the lower Powers do with me as it may please God to suffer them."

The Bishop then said he would like to talk with him further, and requested him to meet him at Tedbury the next day. At the time appointed, Roberts went to the inn where the Bishop lodged, and was invited to dine with him. After dinner was over, the Prelate told him that he must go to church, and leave off holding Conventicles at his house, of which great complaint was made. This he flatly refused to do; and the Bishop, losing patience, ordered the constable to be sent for. Roberts told him, that if, after coming to his house under the guise of friendship, he should betray him and send him to prison, he, who had hitherto commended him for his moderation, would put his name in print, and cause it to stink before all sober people. It was the priests, he told him, who set him on; but, instead of hearkening to them, he should commend them to some honest vocation, and not suffer them to rob their honest neighbors, and feed on the fruits of other men's toil, like caterpillars.

"Whom do you call caterpillars?" cried Priest Rich, of North Surrey.

"We farmers," said Roberts, "call those so who live on other men's fields, and by the sweat of other men's brows; and if thou dost so, thou mayst be one of them."

This reply so enraged the Bishop's attendants, that they could only be appeased by an order for the constable to take him to jail. In fact, there was some ground for complaint of a lack of courtesy on the part of the blunt farmer; and the Christian virtue of forbearance, even in bishops, has its limits.

The constable, obeying the summons, came to the inn, at the door of which the landlady met him. "What do you here!" cried the good woman, "when honest John is going to be sent to prison? Here, come along with me." The constable, nothing loath, followed her into a private room, where she concealed him. Word was sent to the Bishop that the constable was not to be found; and the Prelate, telling Roberts he could send him to jail in the afternoon, dismissed him until evening. At the hour appointed, the latter waited upon the Bishop, and found with him only one priest and a lay gentleman. The priest begged the Bishop to be allowed to discourse with the prisoner; and, leave being granted, he began by telling Roberts that the knowledge of the Scriptures had made him mad, and that it was a great pity he had ever seen them.

"Thou art an unworthy man," said the Quaker, "and I'll not dispute with thee. If the knowledge of the Scriptures has made me mad, the knowledge of the sack-pot hath almost made thee mad; and if we two madmen should dispute about religion, we should make mad work of it."

"An't please you, my Lord," said the scandalized priest, "he says I'm drunk."

The Bishop asked Roberts to repeat his words; and, instead of reprimanding him, as the priest expected, was so much amused that he held up his hands and laughed; whereupon, the offended inferior took a hasty leave. The Bishop, who was evidently glad to be rid of him, now turned to Roberts, and complained that he had dealt hardly with him, in telling him, before so many gentlemen, that he had sought to betray him by professions of friendship, in order to send him to prison; and that, if he had not done as he did, people would have reported him as an encourager of the Quakers. "But now, John," said the good Prelate, "I'll burn the warrant against you before your face." "You know, Mr. Burnet," he continued, addressing his attendant, "that a Ring of Bells may be made of excellent metal, but they may be out of tune; so we may say of John; he is a man of as good metal as I ever met with, but quite out of tune."

"Thou may'st well say so," quoth Roberts, "for I can't tune after thy pipe."

The inferior clergy were by no means so lenient as the Bishop. They regarded Roberts as the Ringleader of Dissent, an impracticable, obstinate, contumacious heretic; not only refusing to pay them tithes himself, but encouraging others to the same course. Hence, they thought it necessary to visit upon him the full rigor of the law. His crops were taken from his field, and his cattle from his yard. He was often committed to the jail, where, on one occasion, he was kept, with many others, for a long time, through the malice of the jailer, who refused to put the names of his prisoners in the Calendar, that they might have a hearing. But the spirit of the old Commonwealth's man remained steadfast. When Justice George, at the Ram in Cirencester, told him he must conform, and go to church, or suffer the penalty of the law, he replied, that he had heard indeed that some were formerly whipped *out* of the Temple, but he had never heard of any being whipped *in*. The Justice, pointing through the open window of the inn, at the church tower, asked him what that was. "Thou may'st call it a daw-house," answered the incorrigible Quaker. "Dost thou not see how the jackdaws flock about it?"

Sometimes it happened that the clergyman was also a magistrate, and united in his own person the authority of the State and the zeal of the Church. Justice Parsons, of Gloucester, was a functionary of this sort. He wielded the sword of the spirit on the Sabbath against Dissenters, and on week days belabored them with the arm of flesh and the constable's staff. At one time he had between forty and fifty of them locked up in Gloucester Castle, among them Roberts and his sons, on the charge of attending Conventicles. But the troublesome prisoners baffled his vigilance, and turned their prison into a meeting-house, and held their Conventicles in defiance of him. The Reverend Justice pounced upon them on one occasion, with his attendants. An old, gray-haired man, formerly a strolling fencing-master, was preaching when he came in. The Justice laid hold of him by his white locks, and strove to pull him down; but the tall fencing-master stood firm and spoke on; he then tried to gag him, but failed in that also. He demanded the names of the prisoners, but no one answered him. A voice (we fancy it was that of our old friend Roberts) called out: "The Devil must be hard put to it to have his drudgery done, when the Priests must leave their pulpits to turn informers against poor prisoners." The Justice obtained a list of the names of the prisoners, made out on their commitment, and, taking it for granted that all were still present, issued warrants for the collection of fines by levies upon their estates. Among the names was that of a poor widow, who had been discharged, and was living, at the time the clerical Magistrate swore she was at the meeting, twenty miles distant from the prison.

Soon after this event, our old friend fell sick. He had been discharged from prison, but his sons were still confined. The eldest had leave, however, to attend him in his illness, and he bears his testimony that the Lord was pleased to favor his father with His living presence in his last moments. In keeping with the sturdy Nonconformist's life, he was interred at the foot of his own orchard, in Siddington; a spot he had selected for a burial-ground long before, where neither the foot of a priest nor the shadow of a steeple-house could rest upon his grave.

In closing our notice of this pleasant old narrative, we may remark that the light it sheds upon the antagonistic religious parties of the time is calculated to dissipate prejudices, and correct misapprehensions, common alike to Churchmen and Dissenters. The genial humor, sound sense, and sterling virtues of the Quaker farmer, should teach the one class that poor James Nayler, in his craziness and folly, was not a fair representative of his sect; while the kind nature, the hearty appreciation of goodness, and the generosity and candor of Bishop Nicholson, should convince the other class that a prelate is not necessarily, and by virtue of his miter, a Laud or a Bonner. The Dissenters of the seventeenth century may well be forgiven for the asperity of their language; men whose ears had been cropped because they would not recognize Charles I as a blessed martyr, and his scandalous son as the head of the Church, could scarcely be expected to make discriminations, or suggest palliating circumstances, favorable to any class of their adversaries. To use the homely but apt simile of McFingal,

> The will's confirmed by treatment horrid,
> As hides grow harder when they're curried.

They were wronged, and they told the world of it. Unlike Shakespeare's cardinal, they did not die without a sign. They branded, by their fierce epithets, the foreheads of their persecutors more deeply than the sheriff's hot iron did their own. If they lost their ears, they enjoyed the satisfaction of making those of their oppressors tingle. Knowing their persecutors to be in the wrong, they did not always inquire whether they themselves had been entirely right, and had done no unrequired works of supererogation by the way of "testimony" against their neighbors' mode of worship. And so from pillory and whipping-post, from prison and scaffold, they set forth their wail and execration, their miserere and anathema, and the sound thereof has reached down to our day. May it never wholly die away until, the world over, the forcing of conscience is regarded as a crime against humanity and a usurpation of God's prerogative. But abhorring, as we must, persecution, under whatever pretext it is employed, we are not therefore to conclude that all persecutors were bad and unfeeling men. Many of their severities, upon which we now look back with horror, were, beyond a question, the result of an intense anxiety for the well-being of immortal souls, endangered by the poison which, in their view, heresy was casting into the waters of life. Coleridge, in one of the moods of a mind which traversed in imagination the vast circle of human experience, reaches this point in his "Table-Talk." "It would require," says he, "stronger arguments than any I have seen to convince me that men in authority have not a right, involved in an imperative duty, to deter those under their control from teaching or countenancing doctrines which they believe to be damnable, and even to punish with death those who violate such prohibition." It would not be very difficult for us to imagine a tender-hearted Inquisitor of this stamp, stifling his weak compassion for the shrieking wretch under bodily torment, by his strong pity for souls in danger of perdition from the sufferer's heresy. We all know with what satisfaction the gentle-spirited Melanchthon heard of the burning of Servetus, and with what zeal he defended it. The truth is, the notion that an intellectual recognition of certain dogmas is the essential condition of salvation lies at the bottom of all intolerance in matters of religion. Under this impression, men are too apt to forget that the great end of Christianity is Love, and that Charity is its crowning virtue; they overlook the beautiful significance of the parable of the heretic Samaritan and the orthodox Pharisee; and thus, by suffering their speculative opinions of the next world to make them uncharitable and cruel in this, they are really the worse for them, even admitting them to be true.

SAMUEL HOPKINS.

THREE quarters of a century ago, the name of Samuel Hopkins was as familiar as a household word throughout New England. It was a spell wherewith to raise at once a storm of theological controversy. The venerable minister who bore it had his thousands of ardent young disciples, as well as defenders and followers of mature age and acknowledged talent; a hundred pulpits propagated the dogmas which he had engrafted on the stock of Calvinism. Nor did he lack numerous and powerful antagonists. The sledge ecclesiastic, with more or less effect, was unceasingly plied upon the strong-linked chain of argument which he slowly and painfully elaborated in the seclusion of his parish. The press groaned under large volumes of theological, metaphysical, and psychological disquisition, the very thought of which is now "a weariness to the flesh"; in rapid succession pamphlet encountered pamphlet, horned, beaked, and sharp of talon, grappling with each other in mid-air, like Milton's angels. That loud controversy, the sound whereof went over Christendom, awakening responses from beyond the Atlantic, has now died away; its watchwords no longer stir the blood of belligerent sermonizers; its very terms and definitions have well-nigh become obsolete and unintelligible. The hands which wrote and the tongues which spoke in that day are now all cold and silent; even Emmons, the brave old intellectual athlete of Franklin, now sleeps with his fathers; the last of the giants. Their fame is still in all the churches; effeminate clerical dandyism still affects to do homage to their memories; the earnest young theologian, exploring with awe the mountainous débris of their controversial lore, ponders over the colossal thoughts entombed therein, as he would over the gigantic fossils of an early creation, and endeavors in vain to recall to the skeleton abstractions before him, the warm and vigorous life wherewith they were once clothed; but Hopkinsianism, as a distinct and living school of philosophy, theology, and metaphysics, no longer exists. It has no living oracles left; and its memory survives only in the doctrinal treatises of the elder and younger Edwards, Hopkins, Bellamy, and Emmons.

It is no part of our present purpose to discuss the merits of the system in question. Indeed, looking at the great controversy which divided New England Calvinism in the eighteenth century, from a point of view which secures our impartiality and freedom from prejudice, we find it exceedingly difficult to get a precise idea of what was actually at issue. To our poor comprehension, much of the dispute hinges upon names rather than things; on the manner of reaching conclusions quite as much as upon the conclusions themselves. Its origin may be traced to the great religious awakening of the middle of the past century, when the dogmas of the Calvinistic faith were subjected to the inquiry of acute and earnest minds, roused up from the incurious ease and passive indifference of nominal orthodoxy. Without intending it, it broke down some of the barriers which separated Arminianism and Calvinism; its product, Hopkinsianism, while it pushed the doctrine of the Genevan reformer on the subject of the Divine decrees and agency to that extreme point where it well-nigh loses itself in Pantheism, held at the same time that guilt could not be hereditary; that man, being responsible for his sinful *acts*, and not for his sinful *nature*, can only be justified by a personal holiness, consisting not so much in legal obedience as in that disinterested benevolence which prefers the glory of God and the welfare of universal being above the happiness of self. It had the merit, whatever it may be, of reducing the doctrines of the Reformation to an ingenious and scholastic form of theology; of bringing them boldly to the test of reason and philosophy. Its leading advocates were not mere heartless reasoners and closet speculators. They taught that sin was selfishness, and holiness self-denying benevolence, and they endeavored to practice accordingly. Their lives recommended their doctrines. They were bold and faithful in the discharge of what they regarded as duty. In the midst of slave-holders, and in an age of comparative darkness on the subject of human rights, Hopkins and the younger Edwards lifted up their voices for the slave. And twelve years ago, when Abolitionism was everywhere spoken against, and the whole land was convulsed with mobs to suppress it, the venerable Emmons, burdened with the weight of ninety years, made a journey to New York, to attend a meeting of the Anti-Slavery Society. Let those who condemn the creed of these men see to it that they do not fall behind them in practical righteousness and faithfulness to the convictions of duty.

Samuel Hopkins, who gave his name to the religious system in question, was born in Waterbury, Conn., in 1721. In his fifteenth year he was placed under the care of a neighboring clergyman, preparatory for college, which he entered about a year after. In 1740, the celebrated Whitefield visited New Haven, and awakened there, as elsewhere, serious inquiry on religious subjects. He was followed the succeeding spring by Gilbert Tennent, the New Jersey revivalist, a stirring and powerful preacher. A great change took place in the college. All the phenomena which President Edwards has described in his account of the Northampton awakening were reproduced among the students. The excellent David Brainard, then a member of the college, visited Hopkins in his apartment, and, by a few plain and earnest words, convinced him that he was a stranger to vital Christianity. In his autobiographical sketch, he describes in simple and affecting language the dark and desolate state of his mind at this period, and the particular exercise which finally afforded him some degree of relief, and which he afterward appears to have regarded as his conversion from spiritual death to life. When he first heard Tennent, regarding him as the greatest as well as the best of men, he made up his mind to study theology with him; but just before the commencement at which he was to take his degree, the elder Edwards preached at New Haven. Struck by the power of the great theologian, he at once resolved to make him his spiritual father. In the winter following, he left his father's house on horseback, on a journey of eighty miles to Northampton. Arriving at the house of President Edwards, he was disappointed by hearing that he was absent on a preaching tour. But he was kindly received by the gifted and accomplished lady of the mansion, and encouraged to remain during the winter. Still doubtful in respect to his own spiritual state, he was, he says, "very gloomy, and retired most of the time in his chamber." The kind heart of his amiable hostess was touched by his evident affliction. After some days she came to his chamber, and, with the gentleness and delicacy of a true woman, inquired into the cause of his unhappiness. The young student disclosed to her, without reserve, the state of his feelings and the extent of his fears. "She told me," says the doctor, "that she had had peculiar exercises respecting me since I had been in the family; that she trusted I should receive light and comfort, and doubted not that God intended yet to do great things by me."

After pursuing his studies for some months with the Puritan philosopher, young Hopkins commenced preaching, and, in 1743, was ordained at Sheffield (now Great Barrington), in the western part of Massachusetts. There were at the time only about thirty families in the town. He says it was a matter of great regret to him to be obliged to settle so far from his spiritual guide and tutor; but seven years after he was relieved and gratified by the removal of Edwards to Stockbridge, as the Indian missionary at that station, seven miles only from his own residence; and for several years the great metaphysician and his favorite pupil enjoyed the privilege of familiar intercourse with each other. The removal of the former in 1758 to Princeton, New Jersey, and his death, which soon followed, are mentioned in the diary of Hopkins as sore trials and afflictive dispensations.

Obtaining a dismissal from his society in Great Barrington in 1769, he was installed at Newport the next year as minister of the First Congregational Church in that place. Newport, at this period was, in size, wealth, and commercial importance, the second town in New England. It was the great slave-mart of the North. Vessels loaded with stolen men and women and children, consigned to its merchant princes, lay at its wharves; immortal beings were sold daily at its market, like cattle at a fair. The soul of Hopkins was moved by the appalling spectacle. A strong conviction of the great wrong of slavery, and of its utter incompatibility with the Christian profession, seized upon his mind. While at Great Barrington, he had himself owned a slave, whom he had sold on leaving the place, without compunction or suspicion in regard to the rightfulness of the transaction. He now saw the origin of the system in its true light; he heard the seamen engaged in the African trade tell of the horrible scenes of fire and blood which they had witnessed, and in which they had been actors; he saw the half-suffocated wretches brought up from their noisome and narrow prison, their squalid countenances and skeleton forms bearing fearful evidence of the suffering attendant upon the transportation from their native homes. The demoralizing effects of slaveholding everywhere forced themselves upon his attention, for the evil had struck its roots deeply in the community, and there were few families into which it had not penetrated. The right to deal in slaves, and use them as articles of property, was questioned by no one; men of all professions, clergymen and church members, consulted only their interest and convenience as to their purchase or sale. The magnitude of the evil at first appalled him; he felt it to be his duty to condemn it, but for a time even his strong spirit faltered and turned pale in contemplation of the consequences to be apprehended from an attack upon it. Slavery and slave trading were at that time the principal source of wealth to the island; his own church and congregation were personally interested in the traffic; all were implicated in its guilt. He stood alone, as it were, in its condemnation ; with here and there an exception, all Christendom maintained the rightfulness of slavery. No movement had yet been made in England against the slave trade ; the decision of Granville Sharp's Somerset case had not yet taken place. The Quakers, even, had not at that time redeemed themselves from the opprobrium. Under these circumstances, after a thorough examination of the subject, he resolved, in the strength of the Lord, to take his stand openly and decidedly on the side of humanity. He prepared a sermon for the purpose, and for the first time, from a pulpit of New England, was heard an emphatic testimony against the sin of slavery. In contrast with the unselfish and disinterested benevolence which formed in his mind the essential element of Christian holiness, he held up the act of reducing human beings to the condition of brutes, to minister to the convenience, the luxury, and lusts of the owner. He had expected bitter complaint and opposition from his hearers, but was agreeably surprised to find that in most cases his sermon only excited astonishment in their minds that they themselves had never before looked at the subject in the light in which he presented it. Steadily and faithfully pursuing the matter, he had the satisfaction to carry with him his church, and obtain from it, in the midst of a slave-holding and slave-trading community, a resolution every way worthy of note in this day of cowardly compromise with the evil, on the part of our leading ecclesiastical bodies:

"*Resolved,* That the slave trade and the slavery of the Africans, as it has existed among us, is a gross violation of the righteousness and benevolence which are so much inculcated in the Gospel, and, *therefore, we will not tolerate it in this church.*"

There are few instances on record of moral heroism superior to that of Samuel Hopkins in thus rebuking slavery in the time and place of its power. Honor to the true man ever, who takes his life in his hands, and, at all hazards, speaks the word which is given him to utter, whether men will hear or forbear, whether the end thereof is to be praise or censure, gratitude or hatred. It well may be doubted, whether, on that Sabbath day, the angels of God, in their wide survey of His universe, looked upon a nobler spectacle than that of the minister of Newport, rising up before his slaveholding congregation and demanding, in the name of the Highest, the "deliverance of the captive and the opening of prison doors to them that were bound."

Dr. Hopkins did not confine his attention solely to slaveholding in his own church and congregation. He entered into correspondence with the early Abolitionists of Europe, as well as his own country. He labored with his brethren in the ministry to bring them to his own view of the great wrong of holding men as slaves. In a visit to his early friend, Dr. Bellamy, at Bethlehem, who was the owner of a slave, he pressed the subject kindly but earnestly upon his attention. Dr. Bellamy urged the usual arguments in favor of slavery. Dr. Hopkins refuted them in the most successful manner, and called upon his friend to do an act of simple justice, in giving immediate freedom to his slave. Dr. Bellamy, thus hardly pressed, said that the slave was a most judicious and faithful fellow; that, in the management of his farm, he could trust everything to his discretion; that he treated him well, and he was so happy in his service that he would refuse his freedom if it were offered him.

"Will you," said Hopkins, "consent to his liberation, if he really desires it?"

"Yes, certainly," said Dr. Bellamy.

"Then let us try him," said his guest.

The slave was at work in an adjoining field, and at the call of his master came promptly to receive his commands.

"Have you a good master?" inquired Hopkins.

"Oh, yes; massa, he berry good."

"But are you happy in your present condition?" queried the Doctor.

"Oh, yes, massa; berry happy."

Dr. Bellamy here could scarcely suppress his exultation at what he supposed was a complete triumph over his anti-slavery brother. But the pertinacious guest continued his queries.

"Would you not be *more* happy if you were free?"

"O, yes, massa," exclaimed the negro, his dark face glowing with new life; "berry much more happy!"

To the honor of Dr. Bellamy, he did not hesitate. "You have your wish," he said to his servant. "From this moment you are free."

Dr. Hopkins was a poor man, but one of his first acts, after becoming convinced of the wrongfulness of slavery, was to appropriate the very sum which, in the days of his ignorance, he had obtained as the price of his slave, to the benevolent purpose of educating some pious colored men in the town of Newport, who were desirous of returning to their native country as missionaries. In one instance he borrowed, on his own responsibility, the sum requisite to secure the freedom of a slave in whom he became interested. One of his theological pupils was Newport Gardner, who, twenty years after the death of his kind patron, left Boston as a missionary to Africa. He was a native African, and was held by Captain Gardner, of Newport, who allowed him to labor for his own benefit, whenever by extra diligence he could gain a little time for that purpose. The poor fellow was in the habit of laying up his small earnings on these occasions, in the faint hope of one day obtaining thereby the freedom of himself and his family. But time passed on, and the hoard of purchase money still looked sadly small. He concluded to try the efficacy of praying. Having gained a day for himself, by severe labor, and communicating his plan only to Dr. Hopkins and two or three other Christian friends, he shut himself up in his humble dwelling, and spent the time in prayer for freedom. Toward the close of the day, his master sent for him. He was told that this was his *gained* time, and that he was engaged for himself. "No matter," returned the master, "I must see him." Poor Newport reluctantly abandoned his supplications, and came at his master's bidding, when, to his astonishment, instead of a reprimand, he received a paper, signed by his master, declaring him and his family from thenceforth free. He justly attributed this signal blessing to the all-wise Disposer, who turns the hearts of men as the rivers of water are turned; but it cannot be doubted that the labors and arguments of Dr. Hopkins with his master were the human instrumentality in effecting it.

In the year 1773, in connection with Dr. Ezra Stiles, he issued an appeal to the Christian community in behalf of the society which he had been instrumental in forming, for the purpose of educating missionaries for Africa. In the desolate and benighted condition of that unhappy continent, he had become painfully interested, by conversing with the slaves brought into Newport. Another appeal was made on the subject in 1776.

The war of the Revolution interrupted, for a time, the philanthropic plans of Dr. Hopkins. The beautiful island on which he lived was at an early period exposed to the exactions and devastations of the enemy. All who could do so, left it for the mainland. Its wharves were no longer thronged with merchandise; its principal dwellings stood empty; the very meeting-houses were in a great measure abandoned. Dr. Hopkins, who had taken the precaution, at the commencement of hostilities, to remove his family to Great Barrington, remained himself until the year 1776, when the British took possession of the island. During the period of its occupation, he was employed in preaching to destitute congregations. He spent the summer of 1777 at Newburyport, where his memory is still cherished by the few of his hearers who survive. In the spring of 1780, he returned to Newport. Everything had undergone a melancholy change. The garden of New England lay desolate. His once prosperous and wealthy church and congregation were now poor, dispirited, and, worst of all, demoralized. His meeting-house had been used as a barrack for soldiers; pulpit and pews had been destroyed; the very bell had been stolen. Refusing, with his characteristic denial of self, a call to settle in a more advantageous position, he sat himself down once more in the midst of his reduced and impoverished parishoners, and, with no regular salary, dependent entirely on such free-will offerings as from time to time were made him, he remained with them until his death.

In 1776 Dr. Hopkins published his celebrated "Dialogue concerning the Slavery of the Africans; showing it to be the Duty and Interest of the American States to Emancipate all their Slaves." This he dedicated to the Continental Congress, the Signers of the Declaration of Independence. It was republished in 1785, by the New York Abolition Society, and was widely circulated. A few years after, on coming unexpectedly into possession of a few hundred dollars, he devoted immediately one hundred of it to the society for ameliorating the condition of the Africans.

He continued to preach until he had reached his eighty-third year. His last sermon was delivered on the sixteenth of the 10th month, 1803, and his death took place in the 12th month following. He died calmly, in the steady faith of one who had long trusted all things in the hand of God. "The language of my heart is," said he, "let God be glorified by all things, and the best interest of His kingdom promoted, whatever becomes of me or my interest." To a young friend, who visited him three days before his death, he said, "I am feeble, and cannot say much. I have said all I can say. With my last words, I tell you, religion is the one thing needful." "And now," he continued, affectionately pressing the hand of his friend, "I am going to die, and I am glad of it." Many years before an agreement had been made between Dr. Hopkins and his old and tried friend, Dr. Hart, of Connecticut, that when either was called home, the survivor should preach the funeral sermon of the deceased. The venerable Dr. Hart accordingly came, true to his promise, preaching at the funeral from the words of Elisha, "My father, my father; the chariots of Israel, and the horsemen thereof." In the burial-ground adjoining his meeting-house lies all that was mortal of Samuel Hopkins.

One of Dr. Hopkins's habitual hearers, and who has borne grateful testimony to the beauty and holiness of his life and conversation, was WILLIAM ELLERY CHANNING. Widely as he afterward diverged from the creed of his early teacher, it contained at least one doctrine to the influence of which the philanthropic devotion of his own life to the welfare of man bears witness. He says himself that there always seemed to him something very noble in the doctrine of disinterested benevolence, the casting of self aside, and doing good irrespective of personal consequences, in this world or another, upon which Dr. Hopkins so strongly insisted, as the all-essential condition of holiness.

How widely apart, as mere theologians, stood Hopkins and Channing! Yet how harmonious their lives and practice! Both could forget the poor interests of self, in view of eternal right and universal humanity. Both could appreciate the saving truth, that love to God and His creation is the fulfilling of the Divine law. The idea of unselfish benevolence, which they held in common, clothed with sweetness and beauty the stern and repulsive features of the theology of Hopkins, and infused a sublime spirit of self-sacrifice and a glowing humanity into the indecisive and less robust faith of Channing. What is the lesson of this, but that Christianity consists rather in the affections than in the intellect; that it is a life, rather than a creed; and that they who diverge the widest from each other in speculation upon its doctrines, may, after all, be found working side by side on the common ground of its practice.

We have chosen to speak of Dr. Hopkins as a philanthropist, rather than as a theologian. Let those who prefer to contemplate the narrow sectarian, rather than the universal man, dwell upon his controversial works, and extol the ingenuity and logical acumen with which he defended his own dogmas and assailed those of others. We honor him, not as the founder of a new sect, but as the friend of all mankind; the generous defender of the poor and oppressed. Great as unquestionably were his powers of argument, his learning, and skill in the use of the weapons of theological warfare; these by no means constitute his highest title to respect and reverence. As the product of an honest and earnest mind, his doctrinal dissertations have at least the merit of sincerity. They were put forth in behalf of what he regarded as truth; and the success which they met with, while it called into exercise his profoundest gratitude, only served to deepen the humility and self-abasement of their author. As the utterance of what a good man believed and felt, as a part of the history of a life remarkable for its consecration to apprehended duty, these writings cannot be without interest even to those who dissent from their arguments, and deny their assumptions. But in the time, now, we trust, near at hand, when distracted and divided Christendom shall unite in a new Evangelical union, in which orthodoxy in life and practice shall be estimated above orthodoxy in theory, he will be honored as a good man, rather than as a successful creed-maker; as a friend of the oppressed, and the fearless rebuker of popular sin, rather than as the champion of a protracted sectarian war. Even now his writings, so popular in their day, are little known. The time may come when no pilgrim of sectarianism shall visit his grave. But his memory will live in the hearts of the good and generous; the emancipated slave shall kneel over his ashes, and bless God for the gift to humanity of a life so devoted to its welfare. To him may be applied the language of one who, on the spot where he labored and laid down to rest, while rejecting the doctrinal views of the theologian, still cherishes the philanthropic spirit of the man:

He is not lost—he hath not passed away—
  Clouds, earths, may pass—but stars shine calmly on;
And he who doth the will of God, for aye
  Abideth, when the earth and heaven are gone;

Alas! that such a heart is in the grave!
  Thanks for the life that now shall never end!
Weep and rejoice, thou terror-hunted slave!
  That hast both lost and found so great a friend!

RICHARD BAXTER.

THE picture drawn by a late English historian of the infamous Jeffreys, in his judicial robes, sitting in judgment upon the venerable Richard Baxter, brought before him to answer to an indictment setting forth that the said "Richardus Baxter, persona seditiosa et factiosa pravæ mentis, impiæ, inquietæ, turbulent disposition et conversation; falso illicte, injuste nequit factiose seditiose, et irreligiose, fecit, composuit, scripsit quendam falsum, seditiosum, libellosum, factiosum et irreligiosum librum," is so remarkable, that the attention of the most careless reader is at once arrested. Who was that old man, wasted with disease, and ghastly with the pallor of imprisonment, upon whom the foul-mouthed buffoon in ermine exhausted his vocabulary of abuse and ridicule? Who was Richardus Baxter?

The author of works so elaborate and profound as to frighten, by their very titles and ponderous folios, the modern ecclesiastical student from their perusal his hold upon the present generation is limited to a few practical treatises, which, from their very nature, can never become obsolete. The "Call to the Unconverted," and "The Saints' Everlasting Rest," belong to no time or sect. They speak the universal language of the wants and desires of the human soul. They take hold of the awful verities of life and death, righteousness and judgment to come. Through them the suffering and hunted minister of Kidderminster has spoken in warning, entreaty, and rebuke, or in tones of tenderest love and pity, to the hearts of the generations which have succeeded him. His controversial works, his confessions of faith, his learned disputations, and his profound doctrinal treatises are no longer read. Their author himself, toward the close of his life, anticipated, in respect to these favorite productions, the children of his early zeal, labor, and suffering, the judgment of posterity. "I perceive," he says, "that most of the doctrinal controversies among Protestants are far more about equivocal words than matter. Experience since the year 1643, to this year, 1675, hath loudly called me to repent of my own prejudices, sidings, and censurings of causes and persons not understood, and of all the miscarriages of my ministry and life which have been thereby caused; and to make it my chief work to call men that are within my hearing to more peaceable thoughts, affections, and practices."

Richard Baxter was born at the village of Eton Constantine, in 1615. He received from officiating curates of the little church such literary instruction as could be given by men who had left the farmer's flail, the tailor's thimble, and the service of strolling stage-players, to perform church drudgery under the Parish incumbent, who was old and well nigh blind. At the age of sixteen, he was sent to a school at Wroxeter, where he spent three years, to little purpose, so far as a scientific education was concerned. His teacher left him to himself mainly, and following the bent of his mind, even at that early period, he abandoned the exact sciences for the perusal of such controversial and metaphysical writings of the schoolmen as his master's library afforded. The smattering of Latin which he acquired only served in after years to deform his treatises with barbarous, ill-adapted, and erroneous citations. "As to myself," said he, in his letter written in old age to Anthony Wood, who had inquired whether he was an Oxonian graduate, "my faults are no disgrace to a university, for I was of none; I have but little but what I had out of books, and inconsiderable help of country divines. Weakness and pain helped me to study how to die; that set me a-studying how to live; and that on studying the doctrine from which I must fetch my motives and comforts; beginning with necessities, I proceeded by degrees, and am now going to see that for which I have lived and studied."

Of the first essays of the young theologian as a preacher of the established Church, his early sufferings from that complicity of diseases with which his whole life was tormented, of the still keener afflictions of a mind whose entire outlook upon life and nature was discolored and darkened by its disordered bodily medium, and of the struggles between his

Puritan temperament and his reverence for Episcopal formulas, much might be profitably said, did the limits we have assigned ourselves admit. Nor can we do more than briefly allude to the religious doubts and difficulties which darkened and troubled his mind at an early period. He tells us at length in his "Life," how he struggled with these spiritual infirmities and temptations. The future life, the immortality of the soul, and the truth of the Scriptures, were by turns questioned. "I never," says he, in a letter to Dr. More, inserted in the *Sadducisimus Triumphatus*, "had so much ado to overcome a temptation as that to the opinion of Averroes, that, as extinguished candles go all out in an illuminated air, so separated souls go all into one common *anima mundi*, and lose their individuation." With these and similar "temptations" Baxter struggled long, earnestly, and in the end triumphantly. His faith, when once established, remained unshaken to the last; and although always solemn, reverential, and deeply serious, he was never the subject of religious melancholy, or of that mournful depression of soul which arises from despair of an interest in the mercy and paternal love of our common Father.

The Great Revolution found him settled as a minister in Kidderminster, under the sanction of a drunken vicar, who, yielding to the clamor of his more sober parishioners, and his fear of their appeal to the Long Parliament, then busy in its task of abating church nuisances, had agreed to give him sixty pounds per year, in the place of a poor, tippling curate, notorious as a common railer and pot-house incumbrance.

As might have been expected, the sharp contrast which the earnest, devotional spirit and painful strictness of Baxter presented to the irreverent license and careless good humor of his predecessor, by no means commended him to the favor of a large class of his parishioners. Sabbath merry-makers missed the rubicund face and maudlin jollity of their old vicar; the ignorant and vicious disliked the new preacher's rigid morality; the better informed revolted at his harsh doctrines, austere life, and grave manner. Intense earnestness characterized all his efforts. Contrasting human nature with the Infinite Purity and Holiness, he was oppressed with a sense of the loathsomeness and deformity of sin, and afflicted by the misery of his fellow-creatures separated from the Divine harmony. He tells us that at this period he preached the terrors of the Law, and the necessity of Repentance, rather than the joys and consolations of the Gospel, upon which he so loved to dwell in his last years. He seems to have felt a necessity laid upon him to startle men from false hope and security, and to call for holiness of life and conformity to the Divine will as the only ground of safety. Powerful and impressive as are the appeals and expostulations contained in his written works, they probably convey but a faint idea of the force and earnestness of those which he poured forth from his pulpit. As he advanced in years, these appeals were less frequently addressed to the fears of his auditors, for he had learned to value a calm and consistent life of practical goodness beyond any passionate exhibition of terrors, fervors, and transports. Having witnessed, in an age of remarkable enthusiasm and spiritual awakening, the ill effects of passional excitements and religious melancholy, he endeavored to present cheerful views of Christian life and duty, and made it a special object to repress morbid imaginations and heal diseased consciences. Thus it came to pass that no man of his day was more often applied to for counsel and relief, by persons laboring under mental depression, than himself. He has left behind him a very curious and not uninstructive discourse, which he entitled "The Cure of Melancholy, by Faith and Physick," in which he shows a great degree of skill in his morbid mental anatomy. He had studied medicine to some extent for the benefit of the poor of his parish, and knew something of the intimate relations and sympathy of the body and mind; he therefore did not hesitate to ascribe many of the spiritual complaints of his applicants to disordered bodily functions; nor to prescribe pills and powders in the place of Scripture texts. More than thirty years after the commencement of his labors at Kidderminster he thus writes: "I was troubled this year with multitudes of melancholy persons from several places of the land; some of high quality, some of low, some exquisitely learned, and some unlearned. I know not how it came to pass, but if men fell melancholy

I must hear from them or see them; more than any physician I knew." He cautions against ascribing melancholy phantasms and passions to the Holy Spirit, warns the young against licentious imaginations and excitements, and ends by advising all to take heed how they make of religion a matter of "fears, tears, and scruples." "True religion," he remarks, "doth principally consist in obedience, love, and joy."

At this early period of his ministry, however, he had all of Whitefield's intensity and fervor, added to reasoning powers greatly transcending those of the revivalist of the next century. Young in years, he was even then old in bodily infirmity and mental experience. Believing himself the victim of a mortal disease, he lived and preached in the constant prospect of death. His *memento mori* was in his bedchamber, and sat by him at his frugal meal. The glory of the world was stained to his vision. He was blind to the beauty of all its "pleasant pictures." No monk of Mount Athos, or silent Chartreuse, no anchorite of Indian superstition, ever more completely mortified the flesh, or turned his back more decidedly upon the "good things" of this life. A solemn and funereal atmosphere surrounded him. He walked in the shadows of the cypress, and literally "dwelt among the tombs." Tortured by incessant pain, he wrestled against its attendant languor and debility as a sinful wasting of inestimable time; goaded himself to constant toil and devotional exercise, and, to use his own words, "stirred up his sluggish soul to speak to sinners with compassion, as a dying man to dying men."

Such entire consecration could not long be without its effect, even upon the "vicious rabble," as Baxter calls them. His extraordinary earnestness, self-forgetting concern for the spiritual welfare of others; his rigid life of denial and sacrifice, if they failed of bringing men to his feet as penitents, could not but awaken a feeling of reverence and awe. In Kidderminster, as in most other parishes of the kingdom, there were at this period pious, sober, prayerful people, diligent readers of the Scriptures, who were derided by their neighbors as Puritans, precisians, and hypocrites. These were naturally drawn toward the new preacher, and he as naturally recognized them as "honest seekers of the word and way of God." Intercourse with such men, and the perusal of the writings of certain eminent Nonconformists, had the effect to abate, in some degree, his strong attachment to the Episcopal formula and polity. He began to doubt the rightfulness of making the sign of the cross in baptism, and to hesitate about administering the sacrament to profane swearers and tipplers.

But while Baxter, in the seclusion of his parish, was painfully weighing the arguments for and against the wearing of surplices, the use of marriage rings, and the prescribed gestures and genuflections of his order; tything, with more or less scruple of conscience, the mint and anise and cummin of pulpit ceremonials, the weightier matters of the law, freedom, justice, and truth, were claiming the attention of Pym and Hampden, Brook and Vane, in the Parliament House. The controversy between King and Commons had reached the point where it could only be decided by the dread arbitrament of battle. The somewhat equivocal position of the Kidderminster preacher exposed him to the suspicion of the adherents of the King and Bishops. The rabble, at that period sympathizing with the party of license in morals and strictness in ceremonials, insulted and mocked him, and finally drove him from his parish.

On the memorable 23d of 10th month, 1642, he was invited to occupy a friend's pulpit at Alcester. While preaching, a low, dull, jarring roll, as of continuous thunder, sounded in his ears. It was the cannon-fire of Edgehill, the prelude to the stern battle-piece of revolution. On the morrow, Baxter hurried to the scene of action. "I was desirous," he says, "to see the field. I found the Earl of Essex keeping the ground, and the King's army facing them on a hill about a mile off. There were about a thousand dead bodies in the field between them." Turning from this ghastly survey, the preacher mingled with the Parliamentary army, when, finding the surgeons busy with the wounded, he very naturally sought occasion for the exercise of his own vocation as a spiritual practitioner. He attached himself to the army. So far as we can gather from his own memoirs, and the testimony of his contemporaries, he was not influenced to this step by any of the political motives which actuated the Parliamentary leaders. He was no Revolutionist. He was as blind and unquestioning in his reverence for the King's person and divine right, and as hearty in his hatred of religious toleration and civil equality, as any of his clerical brethren who officiated in a similar capacity in the ranks of Goring and Prince Rupert. He seems only to have looked upon the soldiers as a new set of parishioners, whom Providence had thrown in his way. The circumstances of his situation left him little choice in the matter. "I had," he says, "neither money nor friends. I knew not who would receive me in a place of safety, nor had I anything to satisfy them for diet and entertainment." He accepted an offer to live in the Governor's house at Coventry, and preach to the soldiers of the garrison. Here his skill in polemics was called into requisition, in an encounter with two New England Antinomians, and a certain Anabaptist tailor who was making more rents in the garrison's orthodoxy than he mended in their doublets and breeches. Coventry seems at this time to have been the rendezvous of a large body of clergymen, who, as Baxter says, were "for King and Parliament"; men who, in their desire for a more spiritual worship, most unwillingly found themselves classed with the sectaries whom they regarded as troublers and heretics, not to be tolerated; who thought the King had fallen into the hands of the Papists, and that Essex and Cromwell were fighting to restore him; and who followed the Parliamentary forces to see to it that they were kept sound in faith, and free from the heresy of which the Court News Book accused them. Of doing anything to overturn the order of Church and State, or of promoting any radical change in the social and political condition of the people, they had no intention whatever. They looked at the events of the time, and upon their duties in respect to them, not as politicians or reformers, but simply as ecclesiastics and spiritual teachers, responsible to God for the religious beliefs and practices of the people, rather than for their temporal welfare and happiness. They were not the men who struck down the solemn and imposing Prelacy of England, and vindicated the divine right of men to freedom by tossing the head of an anointed tyrant from the scaffold at Westminster. It was the so-called schismatics, ranters, and levelers, the disputatious corporals and Anabaptist musketeers, the dread and abhorrence alike of Prelate and Presbyter, who, under the lead of Cromwell,

> Ruined the great work of time,
> And cast the kingdoms old
> Into another mold.

The Commonwealth was the work of the laity, the sturdy yeomanry and God-fearing commoners of England.

The news of the fight of Naseby reaching Coventry, Baxter, who had friends in the Parliamentary forces, wishing, as he says, to be assured of their safety, passed over to the stricken field, and spent a night with them. He was afflicted and confounded by the information which they gave him that the victorious army was full of hot-headed schemers and levelers, who were against King and Church, prelacy and ritual, and who were for a free Commonwealth and freedom of religious belief and worship. He was appalled to find that the heresies of the Antinomians, Arminians, and Anabaptists, had made sadder breaches in the ranks of Cromwell than the pikes of Jacob Astley, or the daggers of the roysterers who followed the mad charge of Rupert. Hastening back to Coventry, he called together his clerical brethren, and told them "the sad news of the corruption of the army." After much painful consideration of the matter, it was deemed best for Baxter to enter Cromwell's army, nominally as its chaplain, but really as the special representative of orthodoxy in politics and religion, against the democratic weavers and prophesying tailors who troubled it. He joined Whalley's regiment, and followed it through many a hot skirmish and siege. Personal fear was by no means one of Baxter's characteristics, and he bore himself through all with the coolness of an old campaigner. Intent upon his single object, he sat unmoved under the hail of cannon-shot from the walls of Bristol, confronted the well-plied culverins of Sherburne, charged side by side with Harrison upon Goring's musketeers at Langford, and heard the exulting thanksgiving of that grim enthusiast, when "with a loud voice he broke forth in praises of God, as one in rapture"; and marched, Bible in hand, with

Cromwell himself, to the storming of Basing-House, so desperately defended by the Marquis of Winchester. In truth, these storms of outward conflict were to him of small moment. He was engaged in a sterner battle with spiritual principalities and powers, struggling with Satan himself in the guise of political levelers and Antinomian sowers of heresy.

No antagonist was too high and none too low for him. Distrusting Cromwell, he sought to engage him in a discussion of certain points of abstract theology, wherein his soundness seemed questionable; but the wary chief baffled off the young disputant by tedious, unanswerable discourses about free grace, which Baxter admits were not unsavory to others, although the speaker himself had little understanding of the matter. At other times, he repelled his sad-visaged chaplain with unwelcome jests, and rough, soldierly merriment; for he had "a vivacity, hilarity, and alacrity, as another man hath when he hath taken a cup too much." Baxter says of him complainingly, "He would not dispute with me at all." But in the midst of such an army, he could not lack abundant opportunity for the exercise of his peculiar powers of argumentation. At Amersham, he had a sort of pitched battle with the contumacious soldiers. "When the public talking day came," says he, "I took the reading pew, and Pitchford's cornet and troopers took the gallery. There did the leader of the Chesham men begin, and afterward Pitchford's soldiers set in and I alone disputed with them from morning until almost night; for I knew their trick, that if I had gone out first, they would have prated what boasting words they listed, and made the people believe that they had baffled me, or got the best; therefore I stayed it out till they first rose and went away." As usual in such cases, both parties claimed the victory. Baxter got thanks only from the King's adherents; "Pitchford's troopers and the leader of the Chesham men" retired from their hard day's work, to enjoy the countenance and favor of Cromwell, as men after his own heart, faithful to the Houses and the Word, against Kingcraft and Prelacy.

Laughed at and held at arm's length by Cromwell, shunned by Harrison and Berry and other chief officers, opposed on all points by shrewd, earnest men, as ready for polemic controversy as for battle with the King's malignants, and who set off against his theological and metaphysical distinctions their own personal experiences and spiritual exercises, he had little to encourage him in his arduous labors. Alone in such a multitude, flushed with victory and glowing with religious enthusiasm, he earnestly begged his brother ministers to come to his aid. "If the army," said he, "had only ministers enough, who could have done such little as I did, all their plot might have been broken, and King, Parliament, and Religion might have been preserved." But no one volunteered to assist him, and the "plot" of Revolution went on.

After Worcester fight he returned to Coventry, to make his report to the ministers assembled there.

He told them of his labors and trials, of the growth of heresy and leveling principles in the army, and of the evident design of its leaders to pull down Church, King, and Ministers. He assured them that the day was at hand when all who were true to the King, Parliament, and Religion should come forth to oppose these leaders, and draw away their soldiers from them. For himself, he was willing to go back to the army, and labor there until the crisis of which he spoke had arrived. "Whereupon," says he, "they all voted me to go yet longer."

Fortunately for the cause of civil and religious freedom, the great body of the ministers, who disapproved of the ultraism of the victorious army, and sympathized with the defeated King, lacked the courage and devotedness of Baxter. Had they promptly seconded his efforts, although the restoration of the King might have been impossible at that late period, the horrors of civil war must have been greatly protracted. As it was, they preferred to remain at home, and let Baxter have the benefit of their prayers and good wishes. He returned to the army with the settled purpose of causing its defection from Cromwell; but, by one of those dispensations which the latter used to call "births of Providence," he was stricken down with severe sickness. Baxter's own comments upon this passage in his life are not without interest. He says God prevented his purposes in his last and chiefest opposition to the army; that he intended to take off or seduce from their officers the regiment with which he was connected, and then to have tried his persuasion upon the others. He says he afterward found that his sickness was a mercy to himself, "for they were so strong and active, and I had been likely to have had small success in the attempt, and to have lost my life among them in their fury." He was right in this last conjecture; Oliver Cromwell would have had no scruples in making an example of a plotting priest; and "Pitchford's soldiers" might have been called upon to silence, with their muskets, the tough disputant who was proof against their tongues.

After a long and dubious illness, Baxter was so far restored as to be able to go back to his old parish at Kidderminster. Here, under the Protectorate of Cromwell, he remained in the full enjoyment of that religious liberty which he still stoutly condemned in its application to others.

He afterward candidly admits, that, under the "Usurper," as he styles Cromwell, "he had such liberty and advantage to preach the Gospel with success, as he could not have under a King, to whom he had sworn and performed true subjection and obedience." Yet this did not prevent him from preaching and printing, "seasonably and moderately," against the Protector. "I declared," said he, "Cromwell and his adherents to be guilty of treason and rebellion, aggravated by perfidiousness and hypocrisy. But yet I did not think it my duty to rave against him in the pulpit, or to do this so unseasonably and imprudently as might irritate him to mischief. And the rather, because, as he kept up his approbation of a godly life in general, and of all that was good, except that which the interest of his sinful cause engaged him to be against. So I perceived that it was his design to do good in the main, and to promote the Gospel and the interests of godliness more than any had done before him."

Cromwell, if he heard of his diatribes against him, appears to have cared little for them. Lords Warwick and Broghill, on one occasion, brought him to preach before the Lord Protector. He seized the occasion to preach against the sectaries, to condemn all who countenanced them, and to advocate the unity of the church. Soon after, he was sent for by Cromwell, who made "a long and tedious speech," in the presence of three of his chief men (one of whom, General Lambert, fell asleep the while), asserting that God had owned his government in a signal manner. Baxter boldly replied to him that he and his friends regarded the ancient monarchy as a blessing, and not an evil, and begged to know how that blessing was forfeited to England, and to whom that forfeiture was made. Cromwell, with some heat, made answer that it was no forfeiture, but that God had made the change. They afterward held a long conference with respect to freedom of conscience, Cromwell defending his liberal policy and Baxter opposing it. No one can read Baxter's own account of these interviews without being deeply impressed with the generous and magnanimous spirit of the Lord Protector in tolerating the utmost freedom of speech on the part of one who openly denounced him as a traitor and usurper. Real greatness of mind could alone have risen above personal resentment under such circumstances of peculiar aggravation.

In the death of the Protector, the treachery of Monk, and the restoration of the King, Baxter and his Presbyterian friends believed that they saw the hand of a merciful Providence preparing the way for the best good of England and the Church. Always royalists, they had acted with the party opposed to the King from necessity rather than choice. Considering all that followed, one can scarcely avoid smiling over the extravagant jubilations of the Presbyterian divines on the return of the royal debauchee to Whitehall. They hurried up to London with congratulations of formidable length and papers of solemn advice and counsel, to all which the careless monarch listened with what patience he was master of. Baxter was one of the first to present himself at Court, and it is creditable to his heart rather than his judgment and discrimination, that he seized the occasion to offer a long address to the King, expressive of his expectation that his Majesty would discountenance all sin and promote godliness, support the true exercise of Church discipline, and cherish and hold up the hands of the faithful ministers of the Church. To all which Charles II "made as gracious an answer as we could expect," says Baxter, "insomuch that old Mr. Ash burst out into tears of joy." Who doubts that the profligate

King avenged himself as soon as the backs of his unwelcome visitors were fairly turned, by coarse jests and ribaldry, directed against a class of men whom he despised and hated, but toward whom reasons of policy dictated a show of civility and kindness.

There is reason to believe that Charles II, had he been able to effect his purpose, would have gone beyond Cromwell himself in the matter of religious toleration ; in other words, he would have taken, in the outset of his reign, the very steps which cost his successor his crown, and procured the toleration of Catholics by a declaration of universal freedom in religion. But he was not in a situation to brave the opposition alike of Prelacy and Presbyterianism, and foiled in a scheme to which he was prompted by that vague, superstitious predilection for the Roman Catholic religion, which at times struggled with his habitual skepticism, his next object was to rid himself of the importunities of sectaries, and the trouble of religious controversies, by re-establishing the liturgy, and bribing or enforcing conformity to it on the part of the Presbyterians. The history of the successful execution of this purpose is familiar to all the readers of the plausible pages of Clarendon on the one side, or the complaining treatises of Neal and Calamy on the other. Charles and his advisers triumphed, not so much through their own art, dissimulation, and bad faith, as through the blind bigotry, divided counsels, and self-seeking of the Nonconformists. Seduction on one hand, and threats on the other, the bribe of bishoprics, hatred of Independents and Quakers, and the terror of penal laws, broke the strength of Presbyterianism.

Baxter's whole conduct, on this occasion, bears testimony to his honesty and sincerity, while it shows him to have been too intolerant to secure his own religious freedom at the price of toleration for Catholics, Quakers, and Anabaptists; and too blind in his loyalty to perceive that pure and undefiled Christianity had nothing to hope for from a scandalous and depraved King, surrounded by scoffing, licentious courtiers, and a haughty, revengeful Prelacy. To secure his influence, the Court offered him the Bishopric of Hereford. Superior to personal considerations, he declined the honor; but somewhat inconsistently, in his zeal for the interests of his party, he urged the elevation of at least three of his Presbyterian friends to the Episcopal bench, to enforce that very liturgy which they condemned. He was the chief speaker for the Presbyterians at the famous Savoy Conference, summoned to advise and consult upon the Book of Common Prayer. His antagonist was Dr. Gunning, ready, fluent, and impassioned. "They spent," as Gilbert Burnet says, "several days in logical arguing, to the diversion of the town, who looked upon them as a couple of fencers, engaged in a discussion which could not be brought to an end." In themselves considered, many of the points at issue seem altogether too trivial for the zeal with which Baxter contested them —the form of a surplice, the wording of a prayer, kneeling at sacrament, the sign of the cross, etc. With him, however, they were of momentous interest and importance, as things unlawful in the worship of God. He struggled desperately, but unavailingly. Presbyterianism, in its eagerness for peace and union, and a due share of State support, had already made fatal concessions, and it was too late to stand upon non-essentials. Baxter retired from the conference baffled and defeated, amid murmurs and jests. "If you had only been as fat as Dr. Manton," said Clarendon to him, "you would have done well."

The Act of Conformity, in which Charles II and his counselors gave the lie to the liberal declarations of Breda and Whitehall, drove Baxter from his sorrowing parishioners of Kidderminster, and added the evils of poverty and persecution to the painful bodily infirmities under which he was already bowed down. Yet his cup was not one of unalloyed bitterness, and loving lips were prepared to drink it with him.

Among Baxter's old parishioners of Kidderminster, was a widowed lady of gentle birth, named Charlton, who, with her daughter Margaret, occupied a house in his neighborhood. The daughter was a brilliant girl, of "strangely vivid wit," and "in early youth," he tells us, "pride, and romances, and company suitable thereunto, did take her up." But ere long, Baxter, who acted in the double capacity of spiritual and temporal physician, was sent for to visit her, on an occasion of sickness. He ministered to her bodily and mental sufferings, and thus secured her gratitude and confidence. On her recovery, under the influence of his warnings and admonitions, the gay young girl became thoughtful and serious, abandoned her light books and companions, and devoted herself to the duties of a Christian profession. Baxter was her counselor and confidant. She disclosed to him all her doubts, trials, and temptations, and he, in return, wrote her long letters of sympathy, consolation, and encouragement. He began to feel such an unwonted interest in the moral and spiritual growth of his young disciple, that, in his daily walks among his parishioners, he found himself inevitably drawn toward her mother's dwelling. In her presence, the habitual austerity of his manner was softened; his cold, close heart warmed and expanded. He began to repay her confidence with his own, disclosing to her all his plans of benevolence, soliciting her services, and waiting, with deference, for her judgment upon them. A change came over his habits of thought and his literary tastes; the harsh, rude disputant, the tough, dry logician, found himself addressing to his young friend epistles in verse on doctrinal points and matters of casuistry; Westminster Catechism in rhyme; the Solemn League and Covenant set to music. A miracle alone could have made Baxter a poet; the cold, clear light of reason "paled the ineffectual fires" of his imagination; all things presented themselves to his vision "with hard outlines, colorless, and with no surrounding atmosphere." That he did, nevertheless, write verses so creditable as to justify a judicious modern critic in their citation and approval, can perhaps be accounted for only as one of the phenomena of that subtle and transforming influence to which even his stern nature was unconsciously yielding. Baxter was in love.

Never did the blind god try his archery on a more unpromising subject. Baxter was nearly fifty years of age, and looked still older. His life had been one long fast and penance. Even in youth he had never known a schoolboy's love for cousin or playmate. He had resolutely closed up his heart against emotions which he regarded as the allurements of time and sense. He had made a merit of celibacy, and written and published against the entanglement of godly ministers in matrimonial engagements and family cares. It is questionable whether he now understood his own case, or attributed to its right cause the peculiar interest which he felt in Margaret Charlton. Left to himself, it is more than probable that he might never have discovered the true nature of that interest, or conjectured that anything whatever of earthly passion or sublunary emotion had mingled with his spiritual Platonism. Commissioned and set apart to preach repentance to dying men, penniless and homeless, worn with bodily pain and mental toil, and treading, as he believed, on the very margin of his grave, what had he to do with love? What power had he to inspire that tender sentiment, the appropriate offspring only of youth, and health, and beauty?

Could any Beatrice see
A lover in such anchorite?

But, in the mean time, a reciprocal feeling was gaining strength in the heart of Margaret. To her grateful appreciation of the condescension of a great and good man—grave, learned, and renowned—to her youth and weakness, and to her enthusiastic admiration of his intellectual powers, devoted to the highest and holiest objects, succeeded, naturally enough, the tenderly suggestive pity of her woman's heart, as she thought of his lonely home, his unshared sorrows, his lack of those sympathies and kindnesses which make tolerable the hard journey of life. Did she not owe to him, under God, the salvation of body and mind? Was he not her truest and most faithful friend, entering with lively interest into all her joys and sorrows? Had she not seen the cloud of his habitual sadness broken by gleams of sunny warmth and cheerfulness, as they conversed together? Could she do better than to devote herself to the pleasing task of making his life happier, of comforting him in seasons of pain and weariness, encouraging him in his vast labors, and throwing over the cold and hard austerities of his nature the warmth and light of domestic affection? Pity, reverence, gratitude, and womanly tenderness, her fervid imagination and the sympathies of a deeply religious nature, combined to influence her decision. Disparity of age and condition rendered it improbable that Baxter would ever venture to address her in any other capacity than that of a friend and teacher; and it was left to herself to give the first intimation of the possibility of a more intimate relation.

It is easy to imagine with what mixed feelings of joy, surprise, and perplexity, Baxter must have received the delicate avowal. There was much in the circumstances of the case to justify doubt, misgiving, and close searchings of heart. He must have felt the painful contrast which that fair girl, in the bloom of her youth, presented to the worn man of middle years, whose very breath was suffering, and over whom death seemed always impending. Keenly conscious of his infirmities of temper, he must have feared for the happiness of a loving, gentle being, daily exposed to their manifestations. From his well-known habit of consulting what he regarded as the Divine Will in every important step of his life, there can be no doubt that his decision was the result quite as much of a prayerful and patient consideration of duty, as of the promptings of his heart. Richard Baxter was no impassioned Abelard; his pupil in the school of his severe and self-denying piety was no Heloise; but what their union lacked in romantic interest was compensated by its purity and disinterestedness, and its sanction by all that can hallow human passion, and harmonize the love of the created with the love and service of the Creator.

Although summoned by a power which it would have been folly to resist, the tough theologian did not surrender at discretion. "From the first thoughts, yet many changes and stoppages intervened and long delays," he tells us. The terms upon which he finally capitulated are perfectly in keeping with his character. "She consented," he says, "to three conditions of our marriage. First, That I should have nothing that before our marriage was hers; that I, who wanted no earthly supplies, might not seem to marry her from selfishness. Second, That she would so alter her affairs that I might be entangled in no lawsuits. Third, That she should expect none of my time which my ministerial work should require."

As was natural, the wits of the Court had their jokes upon this singular marriage; and many of his best friends regretted it, when they called to mind what he had written in favor of ministerial celibacy, at a time when, as he says, "he thought to live and die a bachelor." But Baxter had no reason to regret the inconsistency of his precept and example. How much of the happiness of the next twenty years of his life resulted from his union with a kind and affectionate woman, he has himself testified, in his simple and touching "Breviate of the Life of the late Mrs. Baxter." Her affections were so ardent that her husband confesses his fear that he was unable to make an adequate return, and that she must have been disappointed in him in consequence. He extols her pleasant conversation, her active benevolence, her disposition to aid him in all his labors, and her noble forgetfulness of self in ministering to his comfort in sickness and imprisonment. "She was the meetest helper I could have had in the world," is his language. "If I spoke harshly or sharply, it offended her. If I carried it (as I am apt) with too much negligence of ceremony or humble compliment to any, she would modestly tell me of it. If my looks seemed not pleasant, she would have me amend them (which my weak, pained state of body indisposed me to do)." He admits she had her failings, but, taken as a whole, the "Breviate" is an exalted eulogy.

His history from this time is marked by few incidents of a public character. During that most disgraceful period in the annals of England, the reign of the second Charles, his peculiar position exposed him to the persecutions of Prelacy and the taunts and abuse of the sectaries, standing as he did between these extremes, and pleading for a moderate Episcopacy. He was between the upper millstone of High Church and the nether one of Dissent. To use his own simile, he was like one who seeks to fill with his hand a cleft in a log, and feels both sides close upon him with pain. All parties and sects had, as they thought, grounds of complaint against him. There was in him an almost childish simplicity of purpose, a headlong earnestness and eagerness, which did not allow him to consider how far a present act or opinion harmonized with what he had already done or written. His greatest admirers admit his lack of judgment, his inaptitude for the management of practical matters. His utter incapacity to comprehend rightly the public men and measures of his day is abundantly apparent; and the inconsistencies of his conduct and his writings are too marked to need comment. He suffered persecution for not conforming to some trifling matters of church usage, while he advocated the doctrine of passive obedience to the King or ruling power, and the right of that power to enforce conformity. He wrote against conformity while himself conforming; seceded from the Church, and yet held stated communion with it; begged for the curacy of Kidderminster, and declined the bishopric of Hereford. His writings were many of them directly calculated to make Dissenters from the Establishment, but he was invariably offended to find others practically influenced by them, and quarreled with his own converts to Dissent. The High Churchmen of Oxford burned his "Holy Commonwealth" as seditious and revolutionary; while Harrington and the republican club of Miles's coffee-house condemned it for its hostility to democracy, and its servile doctrine of obedience to kings. He made noble pleas for liberty of conscience, and bitterly complained of his own suffering from Church Courts, yet maintained the necessity of enforcing conformity, and stoutly opposed the tolerant doctrines of Penn and Milton. Never did a great and good man so entangle himself with contradictions and inconsistencies. The witty and wicked Sir Roger L'Estrange compiled from the irreconcilable portions of his works a laughable "Dialogue between Richard and Baxter." The Antinomians found him guilty of Socinianism; and one noted controversialist undertook to show, not without some degree of plausibility, that he was by turns a Quaker and a Papist.

Although able to suspend his judgment and carefully weigh evidence upon matters which he regarded as proper subjects of debate and scrutiny, he possessed the power to shut out and banish at will all doubt and misgiving in respect to whatever tended to prove, illustrate, or enforce his settled opinions and cherished doctrines. His credulity at times seems boundless. Hating the Quakers, and prepared to believe all manner of evil of them, he readily came to the conclusion that their leaders were disguised Papists. He maintained that Lauderdale was a good and pious man, in spite of atrocities in Scotland which entitle him to a place with Claverhouse; and indorsed the character of the infamous Dangerfield, the inventor of the Meal-tub Plot, as a worthy convert from popish errors. To prove the existence of devils and spirits, he collected the most absurd stories and old wives' fables, of soldiers scared from their posts at night by headless bears, of a young witch pulling the hooks out of Mr. Emlen's breeches and swallowing them, of Mr. Beacham's locomotive tobacco-pipe, and the Rev. Mr. Munn's jumping Bible, and of a drunken man punished for his intemperance by being lifted off his legs by an invisible hand! Cotton Mather's marvelous account of his witch experiments in New England delighted him. He had it republished, declaring that "he must be an obstinate Sadducee who doubted it."

The married life of Baxter, as might be inferred from the state of the times, was an unsettled one. He first took a house at Moorfields, then removed to Acton, where he enjoyed the conversation of his neighbor, Sir Matthew Hale; from thence he found refuge in Rickmansworth, and after that in divers other places. "The women have most of this trouble," he remarks, "but my wife easily bore it all." When unable to preach, his rapid pen was always busy. Huge folios of controversial and doctrinal lore followed each other in quick succession. He assailed Popery and the Establishment, Anabaptists, ultra Calvinists, Antinomians, Fifth Monarchy men, and Quakers. His hatred of the latter was only modified by his contempt. He railed rather than argued against the "miserable creatures," as he styled them. They in turn answered him in like manner. "The Quakers," he says, "in their shops, when I go along London streets, say, 'Alas! poor man, thou art yet in darkness.' They have oft come to the congregation, when I had liberty to preach Christ's gospel, and cried out against me as a deceiver of the people. They have followed me home, crying out in the streets, 'The day of the Lord is coming, and thou shalt perish as a deceiver.' They have stood in the market-place, and under my window, year after year, crying to the people, 'Take heed of your priests, they deceive your souls'; and if any one wore a lace or neat clothing, they cried out to me, 'These are the fruits of your ministry.'"

At Rickmansworth, he found himself a neighbor of William Penn, whom he calls "the captain of the Quakers." Ever ready for battle, Baxter encountered him in a public discussion, with such fierceness and bitterness as to force from that mild and amiable civilian the remark that he would rather be Socrates at the final judgment, than Richard Baxter. Both lived to know each other better, and to entertain sentiments of mutual esteem. Baxter himself admits that the Quakers, by their perseverance in holding their religious meetings in defiance of penal laws, took upon themselves the burden of persecution which would otherwise have fallen upon himself and his friends; and makes special mention of the noble and successful plea of Penn before the Recorder's Court in London, based on the fundamental liberties of Englishmen and the rights of the Great Charter.

The intolerance of Baxter toward the Separatists was turned against him whenever he appealed to the King and Parliament against the proscription of himself and his friends. "They gathered," he complains, "out of mine and other men's books all that we had said against liberty for Popery and Quakers railing against ministers in open congregation, and applied it as against the toleration of ourselves." It was in vain that he explained that he was only in favor of a gentle coercion of dissent, a moderate enforcement of conformity. His plan for dealing with sectaries reminds one of old Izaak Walton's direction to his piscatorial readers, to impale the frog on the hook as gently as if they loved him.

While at Acton, he was complained of by Dr. Ryves, the rector, one of the King's chaplains in ordinary, for holding religious services in his family with more than five strangers present. He was cast into Clerkenwell jail, whither his faithful wife followed him. On his discharge he sought refuge in the hamlet of Totteridge, where he wrote and published that Paraphrase on the New Testament which was made the ground of his prosecution and trial before Jeffries.

On the 14th of the 6th month, 1681, he was called to endure the greatest affliction of his life. His wife died on that day, after a brief illness. She who had been his faithful friend, companion, and nurse for twenty years, was called away from him in the time of his greatest need of her ministrations. He found consolation in dwelling on her virtues and excellencies in the "Breviate" of her life; "a paper monument," he says, "erected by one who is following her even at the door in some passion indeed of love and grief." In the preface to his poetical pieces, he alludes to her in terms of touching simplicity and tenderness: "As these pieces were mostly written in various passions, so passion hath now thrust them out into the world. God having taken away the dear companion of the last nineteen years of my life, as her sorrows and sufferings long ago gave being to some of these poems, for reasons which the world is not concerned to know; so my grief for her removal, and the revival of the sense of former things, have prevailed upon me to be passionate in the sight of all."

The circumstances of his trial before the judicial monster, Jeffries, are too well known to justify their detail in this sketch. He was sentenced to pay a fine of five hundred marks. Seventy years of age, and reduced to poverty by former persecutions, he was conveyed to the King's Bench prison. Here for two years he lay a victim to intense bodily suffering. When, through the influence of his old antagonist, Penn, he was restored to freedom, he was already a dying man. But he came forth from prison as he entered it, unsubdued in spirit. Urged to sign a declaration of thanks to James II, his soul put on the athletic habits of youth, and he stoutly refused to commend an act of toleration which had given freedom not to himself alone, but to Papists and Sectaries. Shaking off the dust of the Court from his feet, he retired to a dwelling in Charter-House Square, near his friend Sylvester's, and patiently awaited his deliverance. His death was quiet and peaceful. "I have pain," he said to his friend Mather; "there is no arguing against sense; but I have peace. I have peace." On being asked how he did, he answered, in memorable words, "*Almost well!*"

He was buried in Christ Church, where the remains of his wife and her mother had been placed. An immense concourse attended his funeral, of all ranks and parties. Conformist and Nonconformist forgot the bitterness of the controversialist, and remembered only the virtues and the piety of the man. Looking back on his life of self-denial and faithfulness to apprehended duty, the men who had persecuted him while living wept over his grave. During the last few years of his life, the severity of his controversial tone had been greatly softened; he lamented his former lack of charity, the circle of his sympathies widened, his social affections grew stronger with age, and love for his fellow-men universally, and irrespective of religious differences, increased within him. In his "Narrative," written in the long, cool shadows of the evening of life, he acknowledges with extraordinary candor this change in his views and feelings. He confesses his imperfections as a writer and public teacher. "I wish," he says, "all over-sharp passages were expunged from my writings, and I ask forgiveness of God and man." He tells us that mankind appear more equal to him; the good are not so good as he once thought, nor the bad so evil; and that in all there is more for grace to make advantage of, and more to testify for God and holiness, than he once believed. "I less admire," he continues, "gifts of utterance, and the bare profession of religion, than I once did, and have now much more charity for those who by want of gifts do make an obscurer profession."

He laments the effects of his constitutional irritability and impatience upon his social intercourse and his domestic relations, and that his bodily infirmities did not allow him a free expression of the tenderness and love of his heart. Who does not feel the pathos and inconsolable regret which dictated the following paragraph? "When God forgiveth me, I cannot forgive myself, especially for my rash words and deeds by which I have seemed injurious and less tender and kind than I should have been to my near and dear relations, whose love abundantly obliged me. When such are dead, though we never differed in point of interest or any other matter, every sour or cross or provoking word which I gave them, maketh me almost irreconcilable to myself, and tells me how repentance brought some of old to pray to the dead whom they had wronged to forgive them in the hurry of their passion."

His pride as a logician and skillful disputant abated in the latter and better portion of his life; he had more deference to the judgment of others, and more distrust of his own. "You admire," said he to a correspondent who had lauded his character, "one you do not know; knowledge will cure your error." In his "Narrative" he writes: "I am much more sensible than heretofore of the breadth and length and depth of the radical, universal, odious sin of selfishness, and therefore have written so much against it; and of the excellency and necessity of self-denial and of a public mind, and of loving our neighbors as ourselves." Against many difficulties and discouragements, both within himself and in his outward circumstances, he strove to make his life and conversation an expression of that Christian love, whose root, as he has said with equal truth and beauty,

> ——— is set
> In humble self-denial, undertrod,
> While flower and fruit are growing up to God.*

Of the great mass of his writings, more voluminous than those of any other author of his time, it would ill become us to speak with confidence. We are familiar only with some of the best of his practical works, and our estimate of the vast and appalling series of his doctrinal, metaphysical, and controversial publications, would be entitled to small weight, as the result of very cursory examination. Many of them relate to obsolete questions and issues, monumental of controversies long dead, and of disputatious doctors otherwise forgotten. Yet, in respect to even these, we feel justified in assenting to the opinion of one abundantly capable of appreciating the character of Baxter as a writer. "What works of Mr. Baxter shall I read?" asked Boswell of Dr. Johnson. "Read any of them," was the answer, "for they are all good." He has left upon all the impress of his genius. Many of them contain sentiments which happily find favor with few in our time; philosophical and pyschological disquisitions, which look oddly enough in the light of the intellectual progress of nearly two centuries; dissertations upon evil spirits, ghosts, and witches, which provoke smiles

---

* Poetical Fragments, by R. Baxter, p. 16.

at the good man's credulity; but everywhere we find unmistakable evidences of his sincerity and earnest love of truth. He wrote under a solemn impression of duty, allowing neither pain nor weakness, nor the claims of friendship, nor the social enjoyments of domestic affection, to interfere with his sleepless intensity of purpose. He stipulated with his wife, before marriage, that she should not expect him to relax, even for her society, the severity of his labors. He could ill brook interruption, and disliked the importunity of visitors. "We are afraid, Sir, we break in upon your time," said some of his callers to him upon one occasion. "To be sure you do," was his answer. His seriousness seldom forsook him; there is scarce a gleam of gayety in all his one hundred and sixty-eight volumes. He seems to have relished, however, the wit of others, especially when directed against what he looked upon as error. Marvell's inimitable reply to the High Church pretensions of Parker fairly overcame his habitual gravity, and he several times alludes to it with marked satisfaction; but, for himself, he had no heart for pleasantry. His writings, like his sermons, were the earnest expostulations of a dying man with dying men. He tells us of no other amusement or relaxation than the singing of psalms. "Harmony and melody," said he, "are the pleasure and elevation of my soul. It was not the least comfort that I had in the converse of my late dear wife, that our first act in the morning and last in bed at night was a psalm of praise."

It has been fashionable to speak of Baxter as a champion of civil and religious freedom. He has little claim to such a reputation. He was the stanch advocate of monarchy, and of the right and duty of the State to enforce conformity to what he regarded as the essentials of religious belief and practice. No one regards the Prelates who went to the Tower, under James II, on the ground of conscientious scruples against reading the King's declaration of toleration to Dissenters, as martyrs in the cause of universal religious freedom. Nor can Baxter, although he wrote much against the coercion and silencing of godly ministers, and suffered imprisonment himself for the sake of a good conscience, be looked upon in the light of an intelligent and consistent confessor of liberty. He did not deny the abstract right of ecclesiastical coercion, but complained of its exercise upon himself and his friends as unwarranted and unjust.

One of the warmest admirers and ablest commentators of Baxter designates the leading and peculiar trait of his character as *unearthliness*. In our view, this was its radical defect. He had too little of humanity, he felt too little of the attraction of this world, and lived too exclusively in the spiritual and the unearthly, for a full and healthful development of his nature as a man, or of the graces, charities, and loves of the Christian. He undervalued the common blessings and joys of life, and closed his eyes and ears against the beauty and harmony of outward nature. Humanity, in itself considered, seemed of small moment to him; "passing away" was written alike on its wrongs and its rights, its pleasures and its pains; death would soon level all distinctions; and the sorrows or the joys, the poverty or the riches, the slavery or the liberty of the brief day of its probation seemed of too little consequence to engage his attention and sympathies. Hence, while he was always ready to minister to temporal suffering wherever it came to his notice, he made no efforts to remove its political or social causes. In this respect he differed widely from some of his illustrious contemporaries. Penn, while preaching up and down the land, and writing theological folios and pamphlets, could yet urge the political rights of Englishmen, mount the hustings for Algernon Sydney, and plead for unlimited religious liberty; and Vane, while dreaming of a coming Millennium and Reign of the Saints, and busily occupied in defending his Antinomian doctrines, could at the same time vindicate, with tongue and pen, the cause of civil and religious freedom. But Baxter overlooked the evils and oppressions which were around him, and forgot the necessities and duties of the world of time and sense in his earnest aspirations toward the world of spirits. It is by no means an uninstructive fact, that with the lapse of years his zeal for proselytism, doctrinal disputations, and the preaching of threats and terrors, visibly declined, while love for his fellow-men and catholic charity greatly increased, and he was blessed with a clearer perception of the truth that God is best served through His suffering children, and that love and reverence for visible humanity is an indispensable condition of the appropriate worship of the Unseen God.

But, in taking leave of Richard Baxter, our last words must not be those of censure. Admiration and reverence become us rather. He was an honest man. So far as we can judge, his motives were the highest and best which can influence human action. He had faults and weaknesses, and committed grave errors, but we are constrained to believe that the prayer with which he closes his "Saints' Rest," and which we have chosen as the fitting termination of our article, was the earnest aspiration of his life.

"O merciful Father of Spirits! suffer not the soul of thy unworthy servant to be a stranger to the joys which he describes to others, but keep me, while I remain on earth, in daily breathing after thee, and in a believing affectionate walking with thee! Let those who shall read these pages not merely read the fruits of my studies, but the breathing of my active hope and love; that if my heart were open to their view, they might there read thy love most deeply engraven upon it with a beam from the face of the Son of God; and not find vanity or lust or pride within where the words of life appear without, that so these lines may not witness against me, but proceeding from the heart of the writer, be effectual through thy grace upon the heart of the reader, and so be the savor of life to both."

WILLIAM LEGGETT.

"OH, FREEDOM! thou art not, as poets dream,
A fair young girl, with light and delicate limbs,
And wavy tresses, gushing from the cap
With which the Roman master crowned his slave,
When he took off the gyves. A bearded man,
Armed to the teeth, art thou; one mailed hand
Grasps the broad shield, and one the sword; thy brow,
Glorious in beauty though it be, is scarred
With tokens of old wars; thy massive limbs
Are strong with struggling. Power at thee has launched
His bolts, and with his lightnings smitten thee;
They could not quench the life thou hast from Heaven."
—*Bryant.*

WHEN the noblest woman in all France stood on the scaffold, just before her execution, she is said to have turned toward the statue of Liberty, which strangely enough had been placed near the guillotine, as its patron saint, with the exclamation, "Oh, Liberty! what crimes have been committed in thy name!" It is with a feeling akin to that which prompted this memorable exclamation of Madame Roland, that the sincere lover of human freedom and progress is often compelled to regard American Democracy.

For democracy, pure and impartial; the self-government of the whole; equal rights and privileges, irrespective of birth or complexion; the morality of the Gospel of Christ, applied to legislation; Christianity reduced to practice, and showering the blessings of its impartial love and equal protection upon all, like the rain and dews of heaven—we have the sincerest love and reverence. So far as our own Government approaches this standard—and, with all its faults, we believe it does so more nearly than any other—it has our hearty and steadfast allegiance. We complain of and protest against it only, where, in its original frame-work or actual administration, it departs from the democratic principle. Holding with Novalis, that the Christian religion is the root of all democracy, and the highest fact is the rights of man, we regard the New Testament as the true political text-book; and believe that, just in proportion as mankind receive its doctrines and precepts, not merely as matters of faith, and relating to another state of being, but as practical rules, designed for the regulation of the present life, as well as the future, their institutions, social arrangements, and forms of government, will approximate to the democratic model. We believe in the ultimate complete accomplishment of the mission of Him who came "to preach deliverance to the captive, and the opening of prison doors to them that are bound." We look forward to the universal dominion of His benign humanity; and, turning from the strife and blood, the slavery, and social and political wrongs of the Past and Present, anticipate the realization in the distant Future of that state, when the song of the angels at His advent shall be no longer a prophecy, but the jubilant expression of a glorious reality—"Glory to God in the highest! Peace on earth, and good will to man!"

For the party in this country which has assumed the name of Democracy, as a party, we have had, we confess, for some years past, very little respect. It has advocated many salutary measures, tending to equalize the advantages of trade, and remove the evils of special legislation. But, if it has occasionally lopped some of the branches of the evil tree of oppression, so far from striking at its root, it has suffered itself to be made the instrument of nourishing and protecting it. It has allowed itself to be called, by its Southern flatterers, "THE NATURAL ALLY OF SLAVERY." It has spurned the petitions of the people, in behalf of freedom, under its feet, in Congress and State Legislatures. Nominally the advocate of universal suffrage, it has wrested from the colored citizens of Pennsylvania that right of citizenship, which they had enjoyed under a Constitution framed by Franklin and Rush. Perhaps the most shameful exhibition of its spirit was made in the late Rhode Island struggle, when the free suffrage Convention, solemnly calling heaven and earth to witness its readiness to encounter all the horrors of civil war, in defence of the holy principle of equal and universal suffrage, deliberately excluded colored Rhode Islanders from the privilege of voting. In the Constitutional Conventions of Michigan and Iowa, the same party declared all men equal, and then provided an exception to this rule in the case of the colored inhabitants. Its course on the question of excluding slavery from Texas is a matter of history, known and read of all.

After such exhibitions of its practice, its professions have lost their power. The cant of democracy upon the lips of men who are living down its principles, is, to an earnest mind, well-nigh insufferable. Pertinent were the queries of Eliphaz the Temanite, "Shall a man utter vain knowledge, and fill his belly with the east wind? Shall he reason with unprofitable talk or with speeches, wherewith he can do no good?" Enough of wearisome talk we have had about "progress," the rights of "the masses," the "dignity of labor," and "extending the area of freedom!" "Clear your mind of cant, sir," said Johnsion to Boswell; and no better advice could be now given to a class of our Democratic politicians. Work out your democracy; translate your words into deeds; away with your sentimental generalizations, and come down to the practical details of your duty as men and Christians. What avail your abstract theories, your hopeless virginity of democracy, sacred from the violence of meanings? A democracy which professes to hold, as by divine right, the doctrine of human equality in its special keeping, and which, at the same time, gives its direct countenance and support to the vilest system of oppression on which the sun of heaven looks, has no better title to the name it disgraces than the apostate Son of the Morning has to his old place in heaven. We are using strong language, for we feel strongly on this subject. Let those whose hypocrisy we condemn, and whose sins against humanity we expose, remember that they are the publishers of their own shame, and that they have gloried in their apostasy. There is a cutting severity in the answer which Sophocles puts in the mouth of Electra, in justification of her indignant rebuke of her wicked mother:

> 'Tis you that say it, not I—
> You do the unholy deeds which find me words.

Yet in that party calling itself democratic, we rejoice to recognize true, generous, and thoroughly sincere men; lovers of the word democracy, and doers of it also, honest and hearty in their worship of Liberty, who are still hoping that the antagonism which slavery presents to democracy will be perceived by the people, in spite of the sophistry and appeals to prejudice by which interested partisans have hitherto succeeded in deceiving them. We believe with such that the mass of the democratic voters of the free States are in reality friends of freedom, and hate slavery in all its forms; and that, with a full understanding of the matter, they could never consent to be sold to Presidential aspirants, by political speculators, in lots to suit purchasers, and warranted to be useful in putting down free discussion, perpetuating oppression, and strengthening the hands of modern feudalism. They are beginning already to see that, under the process whereby men of easy virtue obtain offices from the General Government, as the reward of treachery to free principles, the strength and vitality of the party are rapidly declining. To them, at least, democracy means something more than collectorships, consulates, and governmental contracts. For the sake of securing a monopoly of these to a few selfish and heartless party managers, they are not prepared to give up the distinctive principles of democracy, and substitute in their place the doctrines of the Satanic school of politics. They will not much longer consent to stand before the world as the Slavery party of the United States, especially when policy and expediency, as well as principle, unite in recommending a position more congenial to the purposes of their organization, the principles of the fathers of their political faith, the spirit of the age, and the obligations of Christianity.

The death-blow of slavery in this country will be given by the very power upon which it has hitherto relied with so much confidence. Abused and insulted Democracy will, ere long, shake off the loathsome burden under which it is now staggering. In the language of the late Theodore Sedgwick, of Massachusetts, a consistent democrat of the old school, " Slavery, in all its forms, is anti-democratic —an old poison left in the veins, fostering the worst principles of aristocracy, pride, and aversion to labor; the natural enemy of the poor man, the laboring man, the oppressed man. The question is, whether absolute dominion over any creature in the image of man be a wholesome power in a free country; whether this is a school in which to train the young republican mind; whether slave blood and free blood can course healthily together in the same body politic. Whatever may be present appearances, and by whatever name party may choose to call things, this question must finally be settled by the democracy of the country.

This prediction was made eight years ago, at a time when all the facts in the case seemed against the probability of its truth, and when only here and there the voice of an indignant freeman protested against the exulting claims of the slave power upon the democracy as its "natural ally." The signs of the times now warrant the hope of its fulfillment. Over the hills of the East, and over the broad territory of the Empire State a new spirit is moving. Democracy, like Balaam upon Zophim, has felt the divine *afflatus*, and is blessing that which it was summoned to curse.

The present hopeful state of things is owing, in no slight degree, to the self-sacrificing exertions of a few faithful and clear-sighted men, foremost among whom was the late WILLIAM LEGGETT; than whom no one has labored more perseveringly, or, in the end, more successfully, to bring the practice of American democracy into conformity with its professions.

William Leggett! Let our right hand forget its cunning, when that name shall fail to awaken generous emotions, and aspirations for a higher and worthier manhood! True man, and true democrat;

faithful always to liberty, following wherever she led, whether the storm beat in his face or on his back; unhesitatingly counting her enemies his own, whether in the guise of Whig monopoly and selfish expediency, or democratic servility north of Mason and Dixon's line, toward democratic slaveholding south of it; poor, yet incorruptible; dependent upon party favor, as a party editor, yet risking all in condemnation of that party, when in the wrong; a man of the people, yet never stooping to flatter the people's prejudices; he is the politician, of all others, whom we would hold up to the admiration and imitation of the young men of our country. What Fletcher of Saltoun is to Scotland, and the brave spirits of the old Commonwealth time!

> Hands that penned
> And tongues that uttered wisdom, better none—
> The later Sydney, Marvell, Harrington,
> Young Vane, and others, who called Milton friend,

are to England, should Leggett be to America. His character was formed on these sturdy democratic models. Had he lived in their day, he would have scraped with old Andrew Marvell the bare blade-bone of poverty, or even laid his head on the block with Vane, rather than forego his independent thought and speech.

Of the early life of William Leggett we have no very definite knowledge. Born in moderate circumstances, at first a woodsman in the Western wilderness; then a midshipman in the navy; then a denizen of New York, exposed to sore hardships and perilous temptations, he worked his way by the force of his genius to the honorable position of associate editor of the Evening Post, the leading Democratic journal of our great commercial metropolis. Here he became early distinguished for his ultraism in democracy. His whole soul revolted against oppression. He was for liberty everywhere and in all things; in thought, in speech, in vote, in religion, in government, and in trade; he was for throwing off all restraints upon the right of suffrage; regarding all men as brethren, he looked with disapprobation upon attempts to exclude foreigners from the rights of citizenship; he was for entire freedom of commerce; he denounced a national bank; he took the lead in opposition to the monopoly of incorporated banks; he argued in favor of direct taxation, and advocated a free post-office, or a system by which letters should be transported, as goods and passengers now are, by private enterprise. In all this he was thoroughly in earnest. That he often erred through passion and prejudice, cannot be doubted; but in no instance was he found turning aside from the path which he believed to be the true one, from merely selfish considerations. He was honest alike to himself and the public. Every question which was thrown up before him by the waves of political or moral agitation, he measured by his standard of right and truth, and condemned or advocated it, in utter disregard of prevailing opinions, of its effect upon his pecuniary interest, or of his standing with his party. The vehemence of his passions sometimes betrayed him into violence of language and injustice to his opponents; but he had that rare and manly trait which enables its possessor, whenever he becomes convinced of error, to make a prompt acknowledgment of the conviction.

In the summer of 1834, a series of mobs, directed against the abolitionists, who had organized a national society, with the city of New York as its central point, followed each other in rapid succession. The houses of the leading men in the society were sacked and pillaged; meeting-houses broken into and defaced; and the unoffending colored inhabitants of the city treated with the grossest indignity, and subjected, in some instances, to shameful personal outrage. It was emphatically a "Reign of Terror." The press of both political parties and of the leading religious sects, by appeals to prejudice and passion, and by studied misrepresentation of the designs and measures of the abolitionists, fanned the flame of excitement, until the fury of demons possessed the misguided populace. To advocate emancipation, or defend those who did so, in New York, at that period, was like preaching democracy in Constantinople, or religious toleration in Paris on the eve of St. Bartholomew. Law was prostrated in the dust; to be suspected of abolitionism was to incur a liability to an indefinite degree of insult and indignity; and the few and hunted friends of the slave, who, in those nights of terror, laid their heads upon the pillow, did so with the prayer of the Psalmist on their lips, "Defend me from them that rise up against me; save me from bloody men."

At this period the New York Evening Post spoke out strongly in condemnation of the mob. William Leggett was not then an abolitionist; he had known nothing of the proscribed class, save though the cruel misrepresentations of their enemies; but, true to his democratic faith, he maintained the right to discuss the question of slavery. The infection of cowardly fear, which at that time sealed the lips of multitudes, who deplored the excesses of the mob, and sympathized with its victims, never reached him. Boldly, indignantly, he demanded that the mob should be put down at once by the civil authorities. He declared the abolitionists, even if guilty of all that had been charged upon them, fully entitled to the privileges and immunities of American citizens. He sternly reprimanded the board of aldermen of the city, for rejecting with contempt the memorial of the abolitionists to that body, explanatory of their principles, and the measures by which they had sought to disseminate them. Referring to the determination expressed by the memorialists in the rejected document, not to recant or relinquish any principle which they had adopted, but to live and die by their faith, he said: "In this, however mistaken, however mad we may consider their opinions in relation to the blacks, what honest, independent mind can blame them? Where is the man so poor of soul, so white-livered, so base, that he would do less in relation to any important doctrine in which he religiously believed? Where is the man who would have his tenets drubbed into him by the clubs of ruffians, or hold his conscience at the dictation of a mob?"

In the summer of 1835, a mob of excited citizens broke open the post-office at Charleston, South Carolina, and burned in the street such papers and pamphlets as they judged to be "incendiary"; in other words, such as advocated the application of the democratic principle to the condition of the slaves of the South. These papers were addressed not to the slave, but to the master. They contained nothing which had not been said and written by Southern men themselves, the Pinkneys, Jeffersons, Henrys, and Martins of Maryland and Virginia. The example set at Charleston did not lack imitators. Every petty postmaster south of Mason and Dixon's line became ex-officio a censor of the press. The Postmaster-General, writing to his subordinate at Charleston, after stating that the post-office department had "no legal right to exclude newspapers from the mail, or prohibit their carriage or delivery, on account of their character or tendency, real or supposed," declared that he would, nevertheless, give no aid, directly or indirectly, in circulating publications of an incendiary or inflammatory character; and assured the perjured functionary, who had violated his oath of office, that, while he could not sanction, he would not condemn his conduct. Against this virtual encouragement of a flagrant infringement of a constitutional right, this licensing of thousands of petty government officials to sit in their mail offices, to use the figure of Milton, cross-legged, like so many envious Junos, in judgment upon the daily offspring of the press, taking counsel of passion, prejudice, and popular excitement, as to what was " incendiary " or " inflammatory," the Evening Post spoke in tones of manly protest.

While almost all the editors of his party throughout the country, either openly approved of the conduct of the Postmaster-General, or silently acquiesced in it, William Leggett, who, in the absence of his colleague, was at that time sole editor of the Post, and who had everything to lose, in a worldly point of view, by assailing a leading functionary of the government, who was a favorite of the President and a sharer of his popularity, did not hesitate as to the course which consistency and duty required at his hands. He took his stand for unpopular truth, at a time when a different course on his part could not have failed to secure him the favor and patronage of his party. In the great struggle with the Bank of the United States, his services had not been unappreciated by the President and his friends. Without directly approving the course of the Administration on the question of the rights of the abolitionists, by remaining silent in respect to it, he might have avoided all suspicion of mental and moral independence incompatible with party allegiance. The impracticable honesty of Leggett, never bending from the erectness of truth for the sake of that "thrift which follows fawning," dictated a most severe and scorching review of the letter of the Postmaster-General. "More monstrous, more detestable doctrines we have never heard promulgated," he exclaimed, in one of his leading editorials. "With what face after this, can the Postmaster-General punish a postmaster for any exercise of the fearfully dangerous power of stopping and destroying any portion of the mails?" "The abolitionists do not deserve to be placed on the same footing with a foreign enemy, nor their publications as the secret dispatches of a spy. They are American citizens, in the exercise of their undoubted right of citizenship, and however erroneous their views, however fanatic their conduct, while they act within the limits of the law, what official functionary, be he merely a subordinate or the head of the post-office department, shall dare to abridge them of their rights as citizens, and deny them those facilities of intercourse which were instituted for the equal accommodation of all? If the American people will submit to this, let us expunge all written codes, and resolve society into its original elements, where the might of the strong is better than the right of the weak."

A few days after the publication of this manly rebuke, he wrote an indignantly sarcastic article upon the mobs which were at this time everywhere summoned to "put down the abolitionists." The next day, the 4th of the 9th month, 1835, he received a copy of the Address of the American Anti-slavery Society to the public, containing a full and explicit avowal of all the principles and designs of the association. He gave it a candid perusal, weighed its arguments, compared its doctrines with those at the foundation of his own political faith, and rose up from its examination an abolitionist. He saw that he himself, misled by the popular clamor, had done injustice to benevolent and self-sacrificing men; and he took the earliest occasion, in an article of great power and eloquence, to make the amplest atonement. He declared his entire concurrence with the views of the American Anti-slavery Society, with the single exception of a doubt which rested on his mind as to the abolition of slavery in the District of Columbia. We quote from the concluding paragraph of this article:

"We assert without hesitation, that, if we possessed the right, we should not scruple to exercise it for the speedy annihilation of servitude and chains. The impression made in boyhood by the glorious exclamation of Cato,

> A day, an hour, of virtuous liberty,
> Is worth a whole eternity of bondage!

has been worn deeper, not effaced, by time; and we eagerly and ardently trust that the day will yet arrive, when the clank of the bondman's fetters will form no part of the multitudinous sounds which our country sends up to Heaven, mingling, as it were, into a song of praise for our national prosperity.

We yearn with strong desire for the day when freedom shall no longer wave

> Her fustian flag in mockery over slaves.

A few days after, in reply to the assaults made upon him from all quarters, he calmly and firmly reiterated his determination to maintain the right of free discussion on the subject of slavery.

"The course we are pursuing," said he, "is one which we entered upon after mature deliberation, and we are not to be turned from it by a species of opposition, the inefficacy of which we have seen displayed in so many former instances. It is Philip Van Artevelde, who says:

> 'All my life long,
> I have beheld with most respect the man
> Who knew himself, and knew the ways before him;
> And from among them chose considerately,
> With a clear foresight, not a blindfold courage;
> And, having chosen, with a steadfast mind
> Pursued his purpose.'

"This is the sort of character we emulate. If, to believe slavery a deplorable evil and curse, in whatever light it is viewed; if, to yearn for the day which shall break the fetters of three millions of human beings, and restore to them their birthright of equal freedom; if, to be willing, in season and our of season, to do all in our power to promote so desirable a result, by all means not inconsistent with higher duty; if these sentiments constitute us abolitionists, then are we such, and glory in the name." "The senseless cry of 'abolitionist' shall never deter us, nor the more senseless attempt of puny prints to read us out of the democratic party. The often quoted and beautiful saying of the Latin historian, *Homo sum: humani nihil a me alienum puto,* we apply to the poor slave as well as his master, and shall endeavor to fulfill toward both the obligations of an equal humanity."

The generation which, since the period of which we are speaking, have risen into active life, can have but a faint conception of the boldness of this movement on the part of William Leggett. To be an abolitionist then was to abandon all hope of political preferment or party favor; to be marked and branded as a social outlaw, under good society's interdict of food and fire; to hold property, liberty, and life itself at the mercy of a lawless mob. All this William Leggett clearly saw. He knew how rugged and thorny was the path upon which, impelled by his love of truth and the obligations of humanity, he was entering. From hunted and proscribed abolitionists, and oppressed and spirit-broken colored men, the Pariahs of American democracy, he could alone expect sympathy. The Whig journals, with a few honorable exceptions, exulted over what they regarded as the fall of a formidable opponent; and after painting his abolitionism in the most hideous colors, held him up to their Southern allies as a specimen of the radical disorganizers and democratic levelers of the North. His own party, in consequence, made haste to proscribe him. Government advertising was promptly withdrawn from his paper. The official journals of Washington and Albany read him out of the pale of Democracy. Father Ritchie scolded and threatened. The Democratic committee issued its bull against him from Tammany Hall. The resolutions of that committee were laid before him when he was sinking under a severe illness. Rallying his energies, he dictated from his sick bed an answer marked by all his accustomed vigor and boldness. Its tone was calm, manly, self-relying; the language of one who, having planted his feet hard down on the rock of principle, stood there, like Luther at Worms, because he "could not otherwise." Exhausted nature sunk under the effort. A weary sickness of nearly a year's duration followed. In this sore affliction, deserted as he was by most of his old political friends, we have reason to know that he was cheered by the gratitude of those in whose behalf he had well-nigh made a martyr's sacrifice; and that from the humble hearths of his poor colored fellow-citizens fervent prayers went up for his restoration.

His work was not yet done. Purified by trial, he was to stand forth once more in vindication of the truths of freedom. As soon as his health was sufficiently re-established, he commenced the publication of an independent political and literary journal, under the expressive title of THE PLAINDEALER. In his first number he stated that, claiming the right of absolute freedom of discussion, he should exercise it with no other limitations than those of his own judgment. A poor man, he admitted that he established the paper in the expectation of deriving from it a livelihood, but that even for that object he could not trim its sails to suit the varying breeze of popular prejudice. "If," said he, "a paper which makes the Right and not the Expedient its cardinal object will not yield its conductor a support, there are honest vocations that will, and better the humblest of them than to be seated at the head of an influential press, if its influence is not exerted to promote the cause of truth." He was true to his promise. The free soul of a free, strong man spoke out in his paper. How refreshing was it, after listening to the inanities, the dull, witless vulgarity, the wearisome commonplace of journalists who had no higher aim than to echo, with parrot-like exactness, current prejudices and falsehoods, to turn to the great and generous thoughts, the chaste and vigorous diction of the Plaindealer! No man ever had a clearer idea of the duties and responsibilities of a conductor of the public press than William Leggett, and few have ever combined so many of the qualifications for their perfect discharge: a nice sense of justice, a warm benevolence, inflexible truth, honesty defying temptation, a mind stored with learning, and having at command the treasures of the best thoughts of the best authors. As was said of Fletcher of Saltoun, he was "a gentleman steady in his principles, of nice honor, abundance of learning, bold as a lion, a sure friend, a man who would lose his life to serve his country, and would not do a base thing to save it." He had his faults; his positive convictions sometimes took the shape of a proud and obstinate dogmatism; he who could so well appeal to the judgment and the reason of his readers, too often only roused their passions by invective and vehement declamation. Moderate men were startled and pained by the fierce energy of his language; and he not infrequently made implacable enemies of opponents whom he might have conciliated and won over by mild expostulation and patient explanation. It must be urged in extenuation that, as the champion of unpopular truths, he was assailed unfairly on all sides, and indecently misrepresented and calumniated to a degree, as his friend Sedgwick justly remarks, unprecedented even in the annals of the American press, and that his errors in this respect were, in the main, errors of retaliation.

In the Plaindealer, in common with the leading moral and political subjects of the day, that of slavery was freely discussed in all its bearings. It is difficult, in a single extract, to convey an adequate idea of the character of the editorial columns of a paper, where terse and concentrated irony and sarcasm alternate with eloquent appeal and diffuse commentary and labored argument. We can only offer at random the following passages from a long review of a speech of John C. Calhoun, in which that extraordinary man, whose giant intellect has been shut out of its appropriate field of exercise by the very slavery of which he is the champion, undertook to maintain, in reply to a Virginia senator, that chattel slavery was not an evil, but "a great good."

"We have Mr. Calhoun's own warrant for attacking his position with all the fervor which a high sense of duty can give, for we do hold, from the bottom of our soul, that slavery is an evil; a deep, detestable, damnable evil; evil in all its aspects to the blacks, and a greater evil to the whites; an evil moral, social, and political; an evil which shows itself in the languishing condition of agriculture where it exists, in paralyzed commerce, and in the prostration of the mechanic arts; an evil which stares you in the face from uncultivated fields, and howls in your ears through tangled swamps and morasses. Slavery is such an evil that it withers what it touches. Where it is once securely established, the land becomes desolate, as the tree inevitably perishes which the sea-hawk chooses for its nest; while freedom, on the contrary, flourishes, like the tannen, 'on the loftiest and least sheltered rocks,' and clothes with its refreshing verdure what, without it, would frown in naked and incurable sterility.

"If any one desires an illustration of the opposite influences of slavery and freedom, let him look at the two sister States of Kentucky and Ohio. Alike in soil and climate, and divided only by a river, whose translucent waters reveal, through nearly the whole breadth, the sandy bottom over which they sparkle, how different are they in all the respects over which man has control! On the one hand, the air is vocal with the mingled tumult of a vast and prosperous population. Every hill-side smiles with an abundant harvest, every valley shelters a thriving village, the click of a busy mill drowns the prattle of every rivulet, and all the multitudinous sounds of business denote happy activity in every branch of social occupation.

"This is the State which, but a few years ago, slept in the unbroken solitude of nature. The forest spread an interminable canopy of shade over the dark soil on which the fat and useless vegetation rotted at ease, and through the dusky vistas of the wood only savage beasts and more savage men prowled in quest of prey. The whole land now blossoms like a garden. The tall and interlacing trees have unlocked their hold, and bowed before the woodman's ax. The soil is disencumbered of the mossy trunks which had reposed upon it for ages. The rivers flash in the sunlight, and the fields smile with waving harvests. This is Ohio, and this is what *freedom* has done for it.

"Now, let us turn to Kentucky, and note the opposite influences of *slavery*. A narrow and unfrequented path through the close and sultry canebrake conducts us to a wretched hovel. It stands in the midst of an unweeded field, whose dilapidated inclosure scarcely protects it from the lowing and hungry kine. Children half-clad and squalid, and destitute of the buoyancy natural to their age, lounge in the sunshine, while their parent saunters apart, to watch his languid slaves drive the ill-appointed team afield. This is not a fancy picture. It is a true copy of one of the features which make up the aspect of the State, and of every State where the moral leprosy of slavery covers the people with its noisome scales; a deadening lethargy benumbs the limbs of the body politic; a stupor settles on the arts of life; agriculture reluctantly drags the plow and harrow to the field, only when scourged by necessity; the ax drops from the woodman's nerveless hand the moment his fire is scantily supplied with fuel; and the fen, undrained, sends up its noxious exhalations, to rack with cramps and agues the frame already too much enervated by a moral epidemic to creep beyond the sphere of the material miasm."

The Plaindealer was uniformly conducted with eminent ability; but its editor was too far in advance of his contemporaries to find general acceptance, or even toleration. In addition to pecuniary embarrassments, his health once more failed, and in the autumn of 1837 he was compelled to suspend the publication of his paper. One of the last articles which he wrote for it, shows the extent to which he was sometimes carried by the intensity and depth of his abhorrence of oppression, and the fervency of his adoration of liberty. Speaking of the liability of being called upon to aid the master in the subjection of revolted slaves, and in replacing their cast-off fetters, he thus expresses himself: "Would we comply with such a requisition? No! Rather would we see our right arm lopped from our body, and the mutilated trunk itself gored with mortal wounds, than raise a finger in opposition to men struggling in the holy cause of freedom. The obligations of citizenship are strong, but those of justice, humanity, and religion, stronger. We earnestly trust that the great contest of opinion, which is now going on in this country, may terminate in the enfranchisement of the slaves, without recourse to the strife of blood; but should the oppressed bondmen, impatient of the tardy progress of truth, urged only in discussion, attempt to burst their chains by a more violent and shorter process, they should never encounter our arm nor hear our voice in the ranks of their opponents. We should stand a sad spectator of the conflict; and, whatever commiseration we might feel for the discomfiture of the oppressors, we should pray that the battle might end in giving freedom to the oppressed."

With the Plaindealer, his connection with the public, in a great measure, ceased. His steady and intimate friend, personal as well as political, Theodore Sedgwick, Jun., a gentleman who has on many occasions proved himself worthy of his liberty-loving ancestry, thus speaks of him in his private life at this period: "Amid the reverses of fortune, harassed by pecuniary embarrassments, during the tortures of a disease which tore away his life piecemeal, he ever maintained the same manly and unaltered front, the same cheerfulness of disposition, the same dignity of conduct. No humiliating solicitation, no weak complaint, escaped him." At the election in the fall of 1838, the noble-spirited democrat was not wholly forgotten. A strenuous effort, which was well nigh successful, was made to secure his nomination as a candidate for Congress. It was at this juncture that he wrote to a friend in the city, from his residence at New Rochelle, one of the noblest letters ever penned by a candidate for popular favor. The following extracts will show how a true man can meet the temptations of political life:

"What I am most afraid of is, that some of my friends, in their too earnest zeal, will place me in a false position on the subject of slavery. I am an abolitionist. I hate slavery in all its forms, degrees, and influences; and I deem myself bound, by the highest moral and political obligations, not to let that sentiment of hate lie dormant and smoldering in my own breast, but to give it free vent, and let it blaze forth, that it may kindle equal ardor through the whole sphere of my influence. I would not have this fact disguised or mystified for any office the people have it in their power to give. Rather, a thousand times rather, would I again meet the denunciations of Tammany Hall, and be stigmatized with all the foul epithets with which the anti-abolition vocabulary abounds, than recall or deny one tittle of my creed. Abolition is, in my sense, a necessary and a glorious part of democracy; and I hold the right and duty to discuss the subject of slavery, and to expose its hideous evils in all their bearings—moral, social, and political—as of infinitely higher importance than to carry fifty sub-treasury bills. That I should discharge this duty temperately; that I should not let it come in collision with other duties; that I should not let my hatred of slavery transcend the express obligations of the constitution, or violate its clear spirit, I hope and trust you think sufficiently well of me to believe. But what I fear is (not from you, however), that some of my advocates and champions will seek to recommend me to popular support, by representing me as not an abolitionist, which is false. All that I have written, gives the lie to it. All I shall write, will give the lie to it.

"And here, let me add (apart from any consideration already adverted to) that, as a matter of mere policy, I would not, if I could, have my name disjoined from abolitionism. To be an abolitionist now is to be an incendiary; as three years ago, to be an anti-monopolist, was to be a leveler and a Jack Cade. See what three short years have done in effecting the anti-monopoly reform; and depend upon it, that the next three years, or, if not three, say three times three, if you please, will work a greater revolution on the slavery question. The stream of public opinion now sets against us; but it is about to turn, and the regurgitation will be tremendous. Proud in that day may well be the man who can float in triumph on the first refluent wave, swept onward by the deluge which he himself, in advance of his fellows, has largely shared in occasioning. Such be my fate; and, living or dead, it will, in some measure, be mine! I have written my name in ineffaceable letters on the abolition record; and whether the reward ultimately come in the shape of honors to the living man, or a tribute to the memory of a departed one, I would not forfeit my right to it for as many offices as —— has in his gift, if each of them was greater than his own."

After mentioning that he had understood that some of his friends had endeavored to propitiate popular prejudice by representing him as no abolitionist, he says:

"Keep them, for God's sake, from committing any such fooleries for the sake of getting me into Congress. Let others twist themselves into what shapes they please, to gratify the present taste of the people; as for me, I am not formed of such pliant materials, and choose to retain, undisturbed, the image of my God! I do not wish to cheat the people of their votes. I would not get their support, any more than their money, under false pretenses. I am what I am; and, if that does not suit them, I am content to stay at home."

God be praised for affording us, even in these latter days, the sight of an honest man! Amid the heartlessness, the double-dealing, the evasions, the prevarications, the shameful treachery and falsehood of political men of both parties, in respect to the question of slavery, how refreshing is it to listen to words like these! They renew our failing faith in human nature. They reprove our weak misgivings. We rise up from their perusal stronger and healthier. With something of the spirit which dictated them, we renew our vows to freedom, and, with manlier energy, gird up our souls for the stern struggle before us.

As might have been expected, and as he himself predicted, the efforts of his friends to procure his nomination failed; but the same generous appreciators of his rare worth were soon after more successful in their exertions in his behalf. He received from President Van Buren the appointment of the mission to Guatemala; an appointment which, in addition to honorable employment in the service of his country, promised him the advantages of a sea voyage, and a change of climate, for the restoration of his health. The course of Martin Van Buren on the subject of slavery, in the District of Columbia, forms, in the estimation of many of his best friends, by no means the most creditable portion of his political history; but it certainly argues well for his magnanimity and freedom from merely personal resentment, that he gave this appointment to the man who had animadverted upon that course with the greatest freedom, and whose rebuke of the veto pledge, severe in its truth and justice, formed the only discord in the pæan of partisan flattery which greeted his inaugural. But, however well intended, it came too late. In the midst of the congratulations of his friends on the brightening prospect before him, the still hopeful and vigorous spirit of William Leggett was summoned away by death.

Universal regret was awakened. Admiration of his intellectual power, and that generous and full appreciation of his high moral worth, which had been in too many instances withheld from the living man by party policy and prejudice, were now freely accorded to the dead. The presses of both political parties vied with each other in expressions of sorrow at the loss of a great and true man. The Democracy, through all its organs, hastened to canonize him as one of the saints of its calendar. The general committee, in New York, expunged their resolutions of censure. The Democratic Review, at that period the most respectable mouthpiece of the Democratic party, made him the subject of exalted eulogy. His early friend and co-editor, WILLIAM CULLEN BRYANT, laid upon his grave the following tribute, alike beautiful and true:

The earth may ring, from shore to shore,
  With echoes of a glorious name,
But he whose loss our tears deplore
  Has left behind him more than fame.

For when the death-frost came to lie
  On Leggett's warm and mighty heart,
And quenched his bold and friendly eye,
  His spirit did not all depart.

The words of fire that from his pen
  He flung upon the lucid page,
Still move, still shake the hearts of men,
  Amid a cold and coward age.

His love of Truth, too warm, too strong,
For Hope or Fear to chain or chill,
His hate of tyranny and wrong,
Burn in the breasts they kindled still.

So lived and died William Leggett. What a rebuke of party perfidy, of political meanness, of the common arts and stratagems of demagogues, comes up from his grave! How the cheek of mercenary selfishness crimsons at the thought of his incorruptible integrity! How heartless and hollow pretenders, who offer lip service to freedom, while they give their hands to whatever work their slaveholding managers may assign them; who sit in chains round the crib of governmental patronage, putting on the spaniel, and putting off the man, and making their whole lives a miserable lie, shrink back from a contrast with the proud and austere dignity of his character! What a comment on their own condition is the memory of a man who could calmly endure the loss of party favor, the reproaches of his friends, the malignant assaults of his enemies, and the fretting evils of poverty, in the hope of bequeathing, like the dying testator of Ford,

A fame by scandal untouched,
To Memory and Time's old daughter, Truth.

The praises which such men are now constrained to bestow upon him are their own condemnation. Every stone which they pile upon his grave is written over with the record of their hypocrisy.

We have written rather for the living than the dead. As one of that proscribed and hunted band of Abolitionists, whose rights were so bravely defended by William Leggett, we should, indeed, be wanting in ordinary gratitude, not to do honor to his memory; but we have been actuated at the present time mainly by a hope that the character, the lineaments of which we have so imperfectly sketched, may awaken a generous emulation in the hearts of the young democracy of our country. Democracy such as William Leggett believed and practiced, democracy in its full and all-comprehensive significance, is destined to be the settled political faith of this republic. Because the despotism of slavery has usurped its name, and offered the strange incense of human tears and blood on its profaned altars, shall we, therefore, abandon the only political faith which coincides with the Gospel of Jesus, and meets the aspirations and wants of humanity? No. The duty of the present generation in the United States is to reduce this faith to practice; to make the beautiful ideal a fact.

"Every American," says Leggett, "who in any way countenances slavery, is derelict to his duty, as a Christian, a patriot, a man; and every one *does* countenance and authorize it who suffers any opportunity of expressing his deep abhorrence of its manifold abominations to pass unreproved." The whole world has an interest in this matter. The influence of our democratic despotism is exerted against the liberties of Europe. Political reformers in the Old World, who have testified to their love of freedom by serious sacrifices, hold but one language on this point. They tell us that American slavery furnishes kings and aristocracies with their most potent arguments; that it is a perpetual drag on the wheel of political progress.

We have before us, at this time, a letter from Siedensticker, one of the leaders of the patriotic movement in behalf of German liberty in 1831. It was written from the prison of Celle, where he had been confined for eight years. The writer expresses his indignant astonishment at the speeches of John C. Calhoun, and others in Congress, on the slavery question, and deplores the disastrous influence of our great inconsistency upon the cause of freedom throughout the world; an influence which paralyzes the hands of the patriotic reformer, while it strengthens those of his oppressor, and deepens around the living martyrs and confessors of European democracy the cold shadow of their prisons.

Joseph Sturge, of Birmingham, the President of the British Free Suffrage Union, and whose philanthropy and democracy have been vouched for by the Democratic Review in this country, has the following passage in an address to the citizens of the United States: "Although an admirer of the institutions of your country, and deeply lamenting the evils of my own government, I find it difficult to reply to those who are opposed to any extension of the political rights of Englishmen, when they point to America, and say, that where all have a control over the legislation but those who are guilty of a dark skin, slavery and the slave trade remain, not only unmitigated, but continue to extend; and that while there is an onward movement in favor of its extinction, not only in England and France, but in Cuba and Brazil, American legislators cling to this enormous evil, without attempting to relax or mitigate its horrors."

How long shall such appeals, from such sources, be wasted upon us? Shall our baleful example enslave the world? Shall the tree of democracy, which our fathers intended for "the healing of the nations," be to them like the fabled Upas, blighting all around it?

The men of the North, the pioneers of the free West, and the non-slaveholders of the South must answer these questions. It is for them to say whether the present well-nigh intolerable evil shall continue to increase its boundaries, and strengthen its hold upon the government, the political parties, and the religious sects of our country. Interest and honor, present possession and future hope, the memory of fathers, the prospects of children, gratitude, affection, the still call of the dead, the cry of oppressed nations looking hitherward for the result of all their hopes, the voice of God in the soul, in revelation, and in his providence, all appeal to them for a speedy and righteous decision. At this moment, on the floor of Congress, Democracy and Slavery have met in a death-grapple. The South stands firm; it allows no party division on the slave question. One of its members has declared that "the slave States have no traitors." Can the same be said of the free? Now, as in the time of the fatal Missouri compromise, there are, it is to be feared, political peddlers among our representatives, whose souls are in the market, and whose consciences are vendible commodities. Through their means the slave power may gain a temporary triumph; but may not the very baseness of the treachery arouse the Northern heart? By driving the free States to the wall, may it not compel them to turn and take an aggressive attitude, clasp hands over the altar of their common freedom, and swear eternal hostility to slavery?

Be the issue of the present contest what it may, those who are faithful to freedom should allow no temporary reverse to shake their confidence in the ultimate triumph of the right. The slave will be free. Democracy in America will yet be a glorious reality; and when the topstone of that temple of freedom which our fathers left unfinished shall be brought forth with shoutings and cries of grace unto it; when our now drooping liberty lifts up her head and prospers, happy will he be who can say, with John Milton, "Among those who have something more than wished her welfare, I too have my charter and freehold of rejoicing to me and my heirs."

NATHANIEL PEABODY ROGERS.

And Lamb, the frolic and the gentle,
Has vanished from his kindly hearth.

SO, in one of the sweetest and most pathetic of his poems touching the loss of his literary friends, sang Wordsworth. We well remember with what freshness and vividness these simple lines came before us, on hearing, last autumn, of the death of the warm-hearted and gifted friend whose name heads this article; for there was much in his character and genius to remind us of the gentle author of "Elia." He had the latter's genial humor and quaintness; his nice and delicate perception of the beautiful and poetic; his happy, easy diction, not the result, as in the case of that of the English essayist, of slow and careful elaboration, but the natural, spontaneous language in which his conceptions at once embodied themselves, apparently without any consciousness of effort. As Mark Antony talked, he wrote, "right on," telling his readers often what "they themselves did know," yet imparting to the simplest commonplaces of life interest and significance, and throwing a golden haze of poetry over the rough and thorny pathways of everyday duty. Like Lamb, he loved his friends without stint or limit. The "old familiar faces" haunted him. Lamb loved the streets and lanes of London, the places where he oftenest came in contact with the warm, genial heart of humanity, better than the country. Rogers loved the wild and lonely hills and valleys of New Hampshire none the less that he was fully alive to the enjoyments of society, and could enter with the heartiest sympathy into all the joys and sorrows of his friends and neighbors.

In another point of view, he was not unlike Elia. He had the same love of home, and home friends, and familiar objects; the same fondness for common sights and sounds; the same dread of change; the same shrinking from the unknown and the dark. Like him, he clung with a child's love to the living present, and recoiled from a contemplation of the great change which awaits us. Like him, he was content with the goodly green earth, and human countenances, and would fain set up his tabernacle here. He had less of what might be termed self-indulgence in this feeling than Lamb. He had higher views; he loved this world not only for its own sake, but for the opportunities it afforded of doing good. Like the Persian Seer, he beheld the legions of Ormuzd and Ahriman, of Light and Darkness, contending for mastery over the earth, as the sunshine and shadow of a gusty, half-cloudy day struggled on the green slopes of his native mountains; and, mingled with the bright host, he would fain have fought on until its banners waved in eternal sunshine over the last hiding-place of darkness. He entered into the work of reform with the enthusiasm and chivalry of a knight of the crusades. He had faith in human progress, in the ultimate triumph of the good; millennial lights beaconed up all along his horizon. In the philanthropic movements of the day; in the efforts to remove the evils of slavery, war, intemperance, and sanguinary laws; in the humane and generous spirit of much of our modern poetry and literature; in the growing demand of the religious community, of all sects, for the preaching of the Gospel of Love and Humanity, he heard the low and tremulous prelude of the great anthem of Universal Harmony. "The world," said he, in a notice of the music of the Hutchinson family, "is out of tune now. But it will be tuned again, and all will become harmony." In this faith he lived and acted; working, not always, as it seemed to some of his friends, wisely, but bravely, truthfully, earnestly, cheering on his fellow-laborers, and imparting to the dullest and most earthward-looking of them something of his own zeal and loftiness of purpose.

"Who was he?" does the reader ask? Naturally enough, too, for his name has never found its way into fashionable reviews; it has never been associated with tale or essay or poem, to our knowledge. Our friend Griswold, who, like another Noah, has launched some hundreds of American "poets" and prose writers on the tide of immortality in his two huge arks of rhyme and reason, has either overlooked his name, or deemed it unworthy of preservation. Then, too, he was known mainly as the editor of a proscribed and every-where-spoken-against anti-slavery paper. It had few readers of literary taste and discrimination; plain, earnest men and women, intent only upon the thought itself, and caring little for the clothing of it, loved the Herald of Freedom for its honestness and earnestness, and its bold rebukes of the wrong, its all-surrendering homage to what its editor believed to be right. But the literary world of authors and critics saw and heard little or nothing of him or his writings. "I once had a bit of scholarcraft," he says of himself on one occasion, "and had I attempted it in some pitiful sectarian or party or literary sheet, I should have stood a chance to get quoted into the periodicals. Now, who dares quote from the Herald of Freedom?" He wrote for humanity, as his biographer justly says, not for fame. "He wrote because he had something to say, and true to nature; for to him nature was truth; he spoke right on, with the artlessness and simplicity of a child."

He was born in Plymouth, New Hampshire, in the 6th month of 1794; a lineal descendant from John Rogers, of martyr-memory. Educated at Dartmouth College, he studied law with Hon. Richard Fletcher, of Salisbury, New Hampshire, now of Boston, and commenced the practice of it, in 1819, in his native village. He was diligent and successful in his profession, although seldom known as a pleader. About the year 1833 he became interested in the anti-slavery movement. His was one of the few voices of encouragement and sympathy which greeted the author of this sketch on the publication of a pamphlet in favor of immediate emancipation. He gave us a kind word of approval, and invited us to his mountain home, on the banks of the Pemigewasset, an invitation which, two years afterward, we accepted. In the early autumn, in company with George Thompson (the eloquent Reformer, who has since been elected a member of the British Parliament from the Tower Hamlets), we drove up the beautiful valley of the White Mountain tributary of the Merrimac, and, just as a glorious sunset was steeping river, valley, and mountain, in its hues of heaven, were welcomed to the pleasant home and family circle of our friend Rogers. We spent two delightful evenings with him. His cordiality, his warm-hearted sympathy in our object, his keen wit, inimitable humor, and childlike and simple mirthfulness, his full appreciation of the beautiful in art and nature, impressed us with the conviction that we were the guest of no ordinary man; that we were communing with unmistakable genius; such an one as might have added to the wit and eloquence of Ben Jonson's famous club at the Mermaid, or that which Lamb, and Coleridge, and Southey frequented at the "Salutation and Cat," of Smithfield. "The most brilliant man I have met in America!" said George Thompson, as we left the hospitable door of our friend.

In 1838 he gave up his law practice, left his fine outlook at Plymouth upon the mountains of the North, Moose Hillock and the Haystacks, and took up his residence at Concord, for the purpose of editing the Herald of Freedom, an anti-slavery paper which had been started some three or four years before. John Pierpont, than whom there could not be a more competent witness, in his brief and beautiful sketch of the life and writings of Rogers, does not over-estimate the ability with which the Herald was conducted, when he says of its editor: "As a newspaper writer, we think him unequaled by any living man; and in the general strength, clearness, and quickness of his intellect, we think all who knew him well will agree with us, that he was not excelled by any editor in the country." He was not a profound reasoner; his imagination and brilliant fancy played the wildest tricks with his logic; yet, considering the way by which he reached them, it is remarkable that his conclusions were so often correct. The tendency of his mind was to extremes. A zealous Calvinistic church member, he became an equally zealous opponent of churches and priests; a warm politician, he became an ultra non-resistant and no-government man. In all this, his sincerity was manifest. If, in the indulgence of his remarkable powers of sarcasm, in the free antics of a humorous fancy, upon whose graceful neck he had flung loose the reins, he sometimes did injustice to individuals, and touched, in irreverent sport, the hem of sacred garments, it had the excuse, at least, of a generous and honest motive. If he sometimes exaggerated, those who best knew him can testify that he "set down naught in malice."

We have before us a printed collection of his writings: hasty editorials, flung off without care or revision; the offspring of sudden impulse frequently; always free, artless, unstudied; the language transparent as air, exactly expressing the thought. He loved the common, simple dialect of the people—the "beautiful strong old Saxon—the talk words." He had an especial dislike of learned and "dictionary words." He used to recommend Cobbett's Works to "every young man and woman who has been hurt in his or her talk and writing by going to school."

Our limits will not admit of such extracts from the "Collection" of his writings as would convey to our readers an adequate idea of his thought and manner. His descriptions of natural scenery glow with life. One can almost see the sunset light flooding the Franconia Notch, and glorifying the peaks of Moose Hillock, and hear the murmur of the west wind in the pines, and the light, liquid voice of Pemigewasset sounding up from its rocky channel, through its green hem of maples, while reading them. We give a brief extract from an editorial account of an autumnal trip to Vermont:

"We have recently journeyed through a portion of this *free* State; and it is not all imagination in us, that sees, in its bold scenery, its *uninfected* inland position, its mountainous, but fertile and verdant surface, the secret of the noble predisposition of its people. They are *located* for freedom. Liberty's home is on their Green Mountains. Their farmer republic nowhere touches the ocean, the highway of the world's crimes, as well as its nations. It has no seaport for the *importation* of slavery, or the *exportation* of its own highland republicanism. Should slavery ever prevail over this nation, to its utter subjugation, the last lingering footsteps of retiring liberty will be seen, not, as Daniel Webster said, in the proud old Commonwealth of Massachusetts, about Bunker Hill and Faneuil Hall; but she will be found wailing, like Jephthah's daughter, among the 'hollows' and along the sides of the Green Mountains.

"Vermont shows gloriously at this autumn season. Frost has gently laid hands on her exuberant vegetation, tinging her rock-maple woods without abating the deep verdure of her herbage. Everywhere along her peopled hollows and her bold hill-slopes and summits, the earth is alive with green, while her endless *hardwood* forests are *uniformed* with all the hues of early fall, richer than the regimentals of the kings that glittered in the train of Napoleon on the confines of Poland, when he lingered there, on the last outposts of summer, before plunging into the snow-drifts of the North; more gorgeous than the array of Saladin's life-guard in the wars of the crusaders, or of 'Solomon in all his glory,' decked in all colors and hues, but still the hues of life. Vegetation touched, but not dead, or, if killed, not bereft yet of 'signs of life.' 'Decay's effacing fingers' had not yet 'swept the hills' 'where beauty lingers.' All looked fresh as growing foliage. Vermont frosts don't seem to be 'killing frosts.' They only change aspects of beauty. The mountain pastures, verdant to the peaks, and over the peaks of the high steep hills, were covered with the amplest feed, and clothed with countless sheep; the hay-fields heavy with second crop, in some partly cut and abandoned, as if in very weariness and satiety, blooming with honey-suckle, contrasting strangely with the colors on the woods; the fat cattle and the long-tailed colts and the close-built Morgans wallowing in it up to the eyes, or the cattle down to rest, with full bellies, by ten in the morning. Fine but narrow roads wound along among the hills, free almost entirely of stone, and so smooth as to be safe for the most rapid driving, made of their rich, dark, powder-looking soil. Beautiful villages or scattered settlements breaking upon the delighted view on the meandering way, making the ride a continued scene of excitement and animation. The air fresh, free, and wholesome; the road almost dead level for miles and miles, among mountains that lay over the land like the great swells of the sea, and looking in the prospect as though there could be no passage."

To this autumnal limning, the following spring picture may be a fitting accompaniment:

"At last spring is here in full flush. Winter held on tenaciously and mercilessly, but it has let go. The great sun is high on his northern journey, and the vegetation, and the bird-singing, and the loud frog-chorus, the tree budding and blowing are all upon us; and the glorious grass, superbest of earth's garniture, with its ever-satisfying green. The king-birds have come, and the corn-planter, the scolding bob-a-link. 'Plant your corn, plant your corn,' says he, as he scurries athwart the plowed ground, hardly lifting his crank wings to a level with his back, so self-important is he in his admonitions. The earlier birds have gone to housekeeping, and have disappeared from the spray. There has been brief period for them, this spring, for scarcely has the deep snow gone, but the dark-green grass has come, and first we shall know, the ground will be yellow with dandelions.

"I incline to thank Heaven, this glorious morning of May 16th, for the pleasant home from which we can greet the spring. Hitherto we have had to await it amid a thicket of village houses, low down, close together, and awfully white. For a prospect, we had the hinder part of an ugly meeting-house, which an enterprising neighbor relieved us of by planting a dwelling-house right before our eyes (on his own land, and he had a right to), which relieved us also of all prospect whatever. And the revival spirit of habitation which has come over Concord, is clapping up a house between every two in the already crowded town; and the prospect is, it will be soon all buildings. They are constructing, in quite good taste though, small, trim, cottage-like. But I had rather be where I can breathe air, and see beyond my own features, than be smothered among the prettiest houses ever built. We are on the slope of a hill; it is all sand, be sure, on all four sides of us, but the air is free (and the sand, too, at times), and our water, there is danger of hard drinking to live by it. Air and water, the two necessaries of life, and high, free play-ground for the small ones. There is a sand precipice hard by, high enough, were it only rock and overlooked the ocean, to be as sublime as any of the Nahant cliffs. As it is, it is altogether a safer haunt for daring childhood, which could hardly break its neck by a descent of some hundreds of feet.

"A low flat lies between us and the town, with its State-house and body-guard of well-proportioned steeples standing round. It was marshy and wet, but is almost all redeemed by the translation into it of the high hills of sand. It must have been a terrible place for frogs, judging from what remains of it. Bits of water, from the springs hard by, lay here and there about the low ground, which are peopled as full of singers as ever the gallery of the old North Meeting-house was, and quite as melodious ones. Such performers I never heard, in marsh or pool. They are not the great, stagnant, bull paddocks, fat and coarse-noted like Parson ——, but clear-water frogs, green, lively, and sweet-voiced. I passed their orchestra going home the other evening, with a small lad, and they were at it, all parts; ten thousand peeps, shrill, ear-piercing, and incessant, coming up from every quarter, accompanied by a *second*, from some larger swimmer with his trombone, and broken in upon, every now and then, but not discordantly, with the loud quick hallo, that resembles the cry of the tree-toad. 'There are the Hutchinsons,' cried the lad. 'The Rainers,' responded I, glad to remember enough of my ancient Latin, to know that *Rana*, or some such sounding word, stood for frog. But it was a 'band of music,' as the Miller friends say. Like other singers (all but the Hutchinsons) these are apt to sing too much, all the time they are awake, constituting really too much of a good thing. I have wondered if the little reptiles were singing in concert, or whether every one peeped on his own hook, their neighborhood only making it a chorus. I incline to the opinion that they are performing together, that they know the tune, and each carries his part, self-selected, in free meeting, and therefore never discordant. The *hour* rule of Congress might be useful, though far less needed among the frogs than among the profane croakers of the fens at Washington."

Here is a sketch of the mountain scenery of New Hampshire, as seen from the Holderness Mountain, or North Hill, during a visit which he made to his native valley, in the autumn of 1841:

"The earth sphered up all around us, in every quarter of the horizon, like the crater of a vast volcano, and a great hollow within the mountain circle was as smoky as Vesuvius or Etna in their recess of eruption. The little village of Plymouth lay right at our feet, with its beautiful expanse of intervale opening on the eye like a lake among the woods and hills, and the Pemigewasset, bordered along its crooked way with rows of maples, meandering from upland to upland through the meadows. Our young footsteps had wandered over these localities. Time had cast it all far back, that Pemigewasset with its meadows and border trees; that little village whitening in the margin of its intervale; and that one house which we could distinguish, where the mother, that watched over and endured our wayward childhood, totters at four-score.

"To the south stretched a broken, swelling upland country, but champaign from the top of North Hill, patched all over with grain-fields and green wood lots, the roofs of the farmhouses shining in the sun. Southwest, the Cardigan Mountain showed its bald forehead among the smokes of a thousand fires, kindled in the woods in the long drought. Westward, Moose Hillock heaved up its long back, black as a whale; and turning the eye on northward, glancing down the while on the Baker's River valley, dotted over with human dwellings, like shingle bunches for size, you behold the great Franconia Range, its 'Notch' and its Haystacks, the Elephant Mountain on the left, and Lafayette (Great Haystack) on the right, shooting its peak in solemn loneliness high up into the desert sky, and overtopping all the neighboring Alps but Mount Washington itself. The prospect of these is most impressive and satisfactory. We don't believe the earth presents a finer mountain display. The Haystacks stand there like the Pyramids on the wall of mountains. One of them eminently has this Egyptian shape. It is as accurate a pyramid to the eye as any in the old valley of the Nile, and a good deal bigger than any of those hoary monuments of human presumption, of the impious tyranny of monarchs and priests, and of the appalling servility of the erecting multitude. Arthur's Seat in Edinburgh does not more finely resemble a sleeping lion than the huge mountain on the left of the Notch does an elephant, with his great, overgrown rump turned uncivilly toward the gap where the people have to pass. Following round the panorama, you come to the Ossipees and the Sandwich Mountains, peaks innumerable and nameless, and of every variety of fantastic shape. Down their vast sides are displayed the melancholy-looking slides, contrasting with the fathomless woods.

"But the lakes—you see lakes, as well as woods and mountains, from the top of North Hill. Newfound Lake in Hebron, only eight miles distant, you *can't see*, it lies too deep among the hills. Ponds show their small blue mirrors from various quarters of the great picture: Worthen's Mill Pond and the Hardhack, where we used to fish for trout in truant, bare-footed days, Blair's Mill Pond, White Oak Pond, and Long Pond, and the Little Squam, a beautiful, dark sheet of deep, blue water, about two miles long, stretched amid the green hills and woods, with a charming little beach at its eastern end, and without an island. And then the Great Squam, connected with it on the east by a short, narrow stream, the very queen of ponds, with its fleet of islands, surpassing in beauty all the foreign waters we have seen, in Scotland or elsewhere,—the islands covered with evergreens, which impart their hue to the mass of the lake, as it stretches seven miles on east from its smaller sister, toward the peerless Winnipisockee. Great Squam is as beautiful as water and island can be. But Winnipisockee, it is the very 'Smile of the Great Spirit.' It looks as if it had a thousand islands; some of them large enough for little towns, and others not bigger than a swan or a wild duck, swimming on its surface of glass."

His wit and sarcasm were generally too good-natured to provoke even their unfortunate objects, playing all over his editorials like the thunderless lightnings which quiver along the horizon of a night of summer calmness; but at times his indignation launched them like bolts from heaven. Take the following as a specimen. He is speaking of the gag rule of Congress, and commending Southern representatives for their skillful selection of a proper person to do their work:

"They have a quick eye at the South to the character, or, as they would say, the *points* of a slave. They look into him shrewdly, as an old jockey does into a horse. They will pick him out, at rifle-shot distance, among a thousand freemen. They have a nice eye to detect shades of vassalage. They saw in the aristocratic, popinjay strut of a counterfeit Democrat, an itching aspiration to play the slaveholder. They beheld it in 'the cut of his jib,' and his extreme Northern position made him the very tool for their purpose. The little creature has struck at the right of petition. A paltrier hand never struck at a noble right. The Eagle Right of Petition! so loftily sacred in the eyes of the Constitution that Congress can't *begin* to 'ABRIDGE' it, in its pride of place, is hawked at by this crested jay-bird. A 'mousing owl' would have *seen* better at *midnoon*, than to have done it. It is an idiot blue-jay, such as you see fooling about among the scrub oaks and dwarf pitch pines in the winter. What an ignominious death to the lofty right, were it to die by such a hand; but it does not die. It is impalpable to the 'malicious mockery' of such 'vain blows.' We are glad it is done—done by the South—done proudly, and in slaveholding style, by the hand of a vassal. What a man does by another he does by himself, says the maxim. But they will disown the honor of it, and cast it on the despised '*free nigger*' North."

Or this description, not very flattering to the "Old Commonwealth," of the treatment of the agent of Massachusetts in South Carolina:

"Slavery may perpetrate anything, and New England can't see it. It can horsewhip the old Commonwealth of Massachusetts, and spit in her governmental face, and she will not recognize it as an offense. She sent her agent to Charleston on a State embassy. Slavery caught him, and sent him ignominiously home. The solemn great man came back in a hurry. He returned in a most undignified trot. He ran; he scampered—the stately official. The Old Bay State actually pulled foot, cleared, *dug*, as they say, like any scamp with a hue and cry after him. Her grave old senator, who no more thought of having to break his stately walk than he had of being flogged at school for stealing apples, came back from Carolina upon the full run, out of breath, and out of dignity. Well, what's the result? Why, nothing. She no more thinks of showing resentment about it than she would if lightning had struck him. He was sent back 'by the visitation of God'; and if they had lynched him to death, and stained the streets of Charleston with his blood, a Boston jury, if they could have held inquest over him, would have found that he 'died by the visitation of God.' And it would have been 'crowner's quest law,' Slavery's 'crowner's.'"

Here is a specimen of his graceful blending of irony and humor. He is expostulating with his neighbor of the New Hampshire Patriot, assuring him that he cannot endure the ponderous weight of his arguments, begging for a little respite, and, as a means of obtaining it, urging the editor to travel. He advises him to go South, to the White Sulphur Springs, and thinks that, despite of his dark complexion, he would be safe there from being sold for jail fees, as his pro-slavery merits would more than counterbalance his *colored* liabilities, which, after all, were only *prima facie* evidence against him. He suggests Texas, also, as a place where "patriots" of a certain class "most do congregate," and continues as follows:

"There is Arkansas, too, all glorious in new-born liberty, fresh and unsullied, like Venus out of the ocean—that newly discovered star in the firmament banner of this republic. Sister Arkansas, with her bowie-knife graceful at her side, like the huntress Diana with her silver bow; oh, it would be refreshing and recruiting to an exhausted patriot to go and replenish his soul at her fountains. The newly evacuated lands of the Cherokee, too; a sweet place now for a lover of his country to visit, to renew his self-complacency by wandering among the quenched hearths of the expatriated Indians; a land all smoking with the red man's departing curse; a malediction that went to the center. Yes, and Florida—blossoming and leafy Florida, yet warm with life-blood of Osceola and his warriors, shed gloriously under flag of truce. Why should a patriot of such a fancy for nature immure himself in the cells of the city, and forego such an inviting and so broad a landscape? *Ite, viator.* Go forth, traveler, and leave this moldy editing to less elastic fancies. We would respectfully invite our Colonel to *travel.* What signifies? Journey—wander—go forth—itinerate—exercise—perambulate—roam."

He gives the following ludicrous definition of Congress:

"But what is Congress? It is the echo of the country at home; the weathercock, that denotes and answers the shifting wind; a thing of tail, nearly all tail, moved by the tail and by the wind, with small heading, and that corresponding implicitly in movement with the broad sail-like stern, which widens out behind to catch the rum-fraught breath of 'the Brotherhood.' As that turns, it turns; when that stops, it stops; and in calmish weather looks as *steadfast* and *firm* as though it was riveted to the center. The wind blows, and the little popularity-hunting head dodges this way and that, in endless fluctuation. Such is Congress, or a great portion of it. It will point to the northwest heavens of Liberty, whenever the breezes bear down irresistibly upon it, from the regions of political fair weather. It will abolish slavery at the Capitol when it has already been doomed to abolition and death everywhere else in the country. 'It will be in at death.'"

Replying to the charge that the abolitionists of the North were "secret" in their movements and designs, he says:

"'In secret!' Why, our movements have been as prominent and open as the house-tops from the beginning. We have striven from the outset to write the whole matter cloud-high in the heavens, that the utmost South might read it. We have cast an arc upon the horizon, like the semicircle of the polar lights, and upon it have bent our motto, 'IMMEDIATE EMANCIPATION,' glorious as the rainbow. We have engraven it there, on the blue table of the cold vault, in letters tall enough for the reading of the nations. And why has the far South not read and believed before this? Because a steam has gone up, a fog, from New England's pulpit and her degenerate press, and hidden the beaming revelation from its vision. The Northern hierarchy and aristocracy have cheated the South."

He spoke at times with severity of slaveholders, but far oftener of those who, without the excuse of education and habit, and prompted only by a selfish consideration of political or sectarian advantage, apologized for the wrong, and discountenanced the anti-slavery movement. "We have nothing to say," said he, "to the slave. He is no party to his own enslavement, he is none to his disenthrallment. We have nothing to say to the South. The real *holder* of slaves is not there. He is in the North, the free North. The South alone has not the power to hold the slave. It is the character of the nation that binds and holds him. It is the Republic that does it; the efficient force of which is north of Mason and Dixon's line. By virtue of the majority of Northern hearts and voices, slavery lives in the South!"

In 1840 he spent a few weeks in England, Ireland, and Scotland. He has left behind a few beautiful memorials of his tour. His "Ride over the Border," "Ride into Edinburgh," "Wincobank Hall," "Ailsa Craig," gave his paper an interest in the eyes of many who had no sympathy with his political and religious views.

Scattered all over his editorials, like gems, are to be found beautiful images, sweet touches of heartfelt pathos; thoughts which the reader pauses over with surprise and delight. We subjoin a few specimens, taken almost at random from the book before us:

"A thunderstorm—what can match it for eloquence and poetry? That rush from heaven of the big drops, in what multitude and succession, and how they sound as they strike! How they play on the old home roof and the thick tree-tops! What music to go to sleep by, to the tired boy, as he lies under the naked roof! And the great, low bass thunder, as it rolls off over the hills, and settles down behind them to the very center, and you can feel the old earth jar under your feet!"

"There was no oratory in the speech of the Learned Blacksmith, in the ordinary sense of that word; no grace of elocution; but mighty thoughts radiating off from his heated mind, like sparks from the glowing steel of his own anvil."

"The hard hands of Irish labor, with nothing in them—they ring like slabs of marble together, in response to the wild appeals of O'Connell, and the British stand conquered before them, with shouldered arms. Ireland is on her feet, with nothing in her hands, impregnable, unassailable, in utter defenselessness—the first time that ever a nation sprung to its feet unarmed. The veterans of England behold them and forbear to fire. They see no mark. It will not do to fire upon *men*; it will do only to fire upon *soldiers*. *They* are the proper mark of the murderous gun, but *men* cannot be shot."

"It is coming to that (abolition of war) the world over! and when it does come to it, oh! what a long breath of relief the tired world will draw, as it stretches itself for the first time out upon earth's greensward, and learns the meaning of repose and peaceful sleep!"

"He who vests his labor in the faithful ground is dealing directly with God; human fraud or weakness does not intervene between him and his requital. No mechanic has a set of customers so trustworthy as God and the elements. No savings bank is so sure as the old earth."

"Literature is the luxury of words. It originates nothing, it does nothing. It talks hard words about the labor of others, and is reckoned more meritorious for it than genius and labor for *doing* what learning can only descant upon. It trades on the capital of unlettered minds. It struts in stolen plumage, and it is mere plumage. A learned man resembles an owl in more respects than the matter of wisdom. Like that solemn bird, he is about all feathers."

"Our Second Advent friends contemplate a grand conflagration about the first of April next. I should be willing there should be one, if it could be confined to the productions of the press with which the earth is absolutely smothered. Humanity wants precious few books to read, but the great living, breathing, immortal volume of Providence. Life—real life—how to live, how to treat one another, and how to trust God in matters beyond our ken and occasion—these are the lessons to learn, and you find little of them in libraries."

"That accursed drum and fife! How they have maddened mankind! And the deep bass boom of the cannon, chiming in in the chorus of battle—that trumpet and wild charging bugle, how they set the military devil in a man, and make him into a soldier! Think of the human family falling upon one another at the inspiration of music! How must God feel at it! to see those harp-strings He meant should be waked to a love bordering on divine, strung and swept to mortal hate and butchery!"

"Leave off being Jews [he is addressing Major Noah with regard to his appeal to his brethren to return to Judea], and turn *mankind.* The rocks and sands of Palestine have been worshiped long enough. Connecticut River and the Merrimac are as good rivers as any Jordan that ever run into a dead or live sea, and as holy, for that matter. In Humanity, as in Christ Jesus, as Paul says, 'there is neither Jew nor Greek.' And there ought to be none. Let Humanity be reverenced with the tenderest devotion; suffering, discouraged, down-trodden, hard-handed, haggard-eyed, care-worn mankind! Let these be regarded a little. Would to God I could alleviate all their sorrows, and leave them a chance to laugh! They are miserable now. They might be as happy as the blackbird on the spray, and as full of melody."

"I am sick as death at this miserable struggle among mankind for a living. Poor devils! were they born to run such a gauntlet after the means of life? Look about you, and see your squirming neighbors, writhing and twisting like so many angle-worms in a fisher's bait-box, or the wriggling animalculæ seen in the vinegar-drop held to the sun. How they look, how they feel, how base it makes them all!"

"Every human being is entitled to the means of life, as the trout is to his brook, or the lark to the blue sky. Is it well to put a human 'young one' here to die of hunger, thirst and nakedness, or else be preserved as a *pauper?* Is this fair earth but a poor-house by creation and intent? Was it made for that?—and these other round things we see dancing in the firmament to the music of the spheres, are they all great shining poor-houses?"

"The divines always admit things after the age has adopted them. They are as careful of the age as the weathercock is of the wind. You might as well catch an old experienced weathercock, on some ancient orthodox steeple, standing all day with its tail east in a strong out wind, as the divines at odds with the age."

But we must cease quoting. The admirers of Jean Paul Richter might find much of the charm and variety of the "Flower, Fruit, and Thorn Pieces," in this newspaper collection. They may see, perhaps, as we do, some things which they cannot approve of, the tendency of which, however intended, is very questionable. But, with us, they will pardon something to the spirit of Liberty—

much to that of Love and Humanity which breathes through all.

Disgusted and heartsick at the general indifference of church and clergy to the temporal condition of the people, at their apologies for and defenses of slavery, war, and capital punishment, Rogers turned *Protestant*, in the full sense of the term. He spoke of priests and "pulpit wizards" as freely as John Milton did two centuries ago, although with far less bitterness and rasping satire. He could not endure to see Christianity and Humanity divorced. He longed to see the beautiful life of Jesus—his sweet humanities, his brotherly love, his abounding sympathies—made the example of all men. Thoroughly democratic, in his view all men were equal. Priests, stripped of their sacerdotal tailoring, were in his view but men, after all. He pitied them, he said, for they were in a wrong position, above life's comforts and sympathies, "up in the unnatural cold, they had better come down among men, and endure and enjoy with them." "Mankind," said he, "want the healing influences of Humanity. They must love one another more. Disinterested good will make the world as it should be."

His last visit to his native valley was in the autumn of 1845. In a familiar letter to a friend, he thus describes his farewell view of the mountain glories of his childhood's home:

"I went a jaunt, Thursday last, about twenty miles north of this valley, into the mountain region, where, what I beheld, if I could tell it as I saw it, would make your outlawed sheet sought after wherever our Anglo-Saxon tongue is spoken in the wide world. I have been many a time among those Alps, and never without a kindling of wildest enthusiasm in my woodland blood. But I never *saw them* till last Thursday. They never loomed distinctly to my eye *before*, and the sun never *shone on them* from heaven *till then*. They were so near me I could seem to hear the voice of their cataracts, as I could count their great slides, streaming adown their lone and desolate sides. Old slides some of them, overgrown with young woods, like half-healed scars on the breast of a giant. The great rains had clothed the valleys of the upper Pemigewasset in the darkest and deepest green. The meadows were richer and more glorious, in their thick 'fall feed,' than 'Queen Anne's Garden,' as I saw it from the windows of Windsor Castle. And the dark hemlock and hackmatack woods were yet darker after the wet season, as they lay, in a hundred wildernesses, in the mighty recesses of the mountains. But the Peaks—the eternal, the solitary, the beautiful, the glorious and dear mountain peaks, my own Moose Hillock and my native 'Haystacks'—these were the things on which eye and heart gazed and lingered, and I seemed to see them for the last time. It was on my way back that I halted and turned to look at them, from a high point on the Thornton road. It was about four in the afternoon. It had rained among the hills about the 'Notch,' and cleared off. The sun, there sombered, at that early hour, as toward his setting, was pouring his most glorious light upon the naked Peaks, and they casting their mighty shadows far down among the inaccessible woods that darken the hollows that stretch between their bases. A cloud was creeping up to perch and rest a while on the highest top of 'Great Haystack.' Vulgar folks have called it *Mount Lafayette*, since the visit of that brave old Frenchman, in '25 or '26. If they had asked his opinion, he would have told them the names of mountains couldn't be altered, and especially names like that, so appropriate, so descriptive, and so picturesque. A little, hard, white cloud, that looked like a hundred fleeces of wool rolled into one, was climbing rapidly along up the northwestern ridge, that ascended to the lonely top of 'Great Haystack.' All the others were bare. Four or five of them, as distinct and shapely as so many pyramids, some topped out with naked cliff, on which the sun lay in melancholy glory; others clothed thick all the way up with the old New Hampshire hemlock, or the daring hackmatack, Pierpont's hackmatack. You could see their shadows stretching many and many a mile, over 'Grant' and 'Location,' away beyond the invading foot of Incorporation; where the timber-hunter has scarcely explored, and where the moose browses now, I suppose, as undisturbed as he did before the settlement of the State. I wish our young friend and genius, Harrison Eastman, had been with me, to see the sunlight, as it glared on the tops of those woods, and to see the purple of the mountains. I looked at it, myself, almost with the eye of a painter. If a painter looked with mine, though, he never could look off, upon his canvas, long enough to make a picture; he would gaze forever at the original.

"But I had to leave it, and to say in my heart, farewell! And as I traveled on down, and the sun sunk lower and lower toward the summit of the western ridge, the clouds came up and formed an Alpine range in the evening heavens, above it, like other Haystacks and Moose Hillocks, so dark and dense, that fancy could easily mistake them for a higher Alps. There were the peaks, and the great passes; the Franconia 'Notches' among the cloudy cliffs, and the great White Mountain 'Gap.'"

His health, never robust, had been gradually failing for some time previous to his death. He needed more repose and quiet than his duties as an editor left him; and to this end he purchased a small and pleasant farm in his loved Pemigewasset valley, in the hope that he might there recruit his wasted energies. In the 6th month of the year of his death, in a letter to us, he spoke of his prospects in language which even then brought moisture to our eyes:

"I am striving to get me an asylum of a farm. I have a wife and seven children, every one of them with a whole spirit. I don't want to be separated from any of them, only with a view to come together again. I have a beautiful little retreat in prospect, forty odd miles north, where I imagine I can get potatoes and repose—a sort of haven or port. I am among the breakers, and 'mad for land.' If I get this home—it is a mile or two in among the hills from the pretty domicile once visited by yourself and glorious Thompson—I am this moment indulging the fancy that I may see you at it before we die. Why can't I have you come and see me? You see, dear W., I don't want to send you anything short of a full epistle. Let me end as I begun, with the proffer of my hand in grasp of yours extended. My heart I do not proffer—it was yours before—it *shall* be yours while I am "N. P. ROGERS."

Alas! the haven of a deeper repose than he had dreamed of was close at hand. He lingered until the middle of the 10th month, suffering much, yet calm and sensible to the last. Just before his death, he desired his children to sing at his bed-side that touching song of Lover's "The Angel's Whisper." Turning his eyes toward the open window, through which the leafy glory of the season he most loved was visible, he listened to the sweet melody. In the words of his friend Pierpont:

The Angel's whisper stole in song upon his closing ear;
From his own daughter's lips it came, so musical and clear,
That scarcely knew the dying man what melody was there—
The last of earth's or first of heaven's pervading all the air.

He sleeps in the Concord burial-ground, under the shadow of oaks; the very spot he would have chosen, for he looked upon trees with something akin to human affection. "They are," he said, "the beautiful handiwork and architecture of God, on which the eye never tires. Every one is 'a feather in the earth's cap,' a plume in her bonnet, a tress on her forehead—a comfort, a refreshing, and an ornament to her." Spring has hung over him her buds, and opened beside him her violets. Summer has laid her green oaken garland on his grave, and now the frost-blooms of autumn drop upon it. Shall man cast a nettle on that mound? He loved Humanity—shall *it* be less kind to him than Nature? Shall the bigotry of sect, and creed, and profession, drive its condemnatory stake into his grave? God forbid. The doubts which he sometimes unguardedly expressed had relation, we are constrained to believe, to the glosses of commentators and creed-makers, and the inconsistency of professors, rather than to those facts and precepts of Christianity, to which he gave the constant assent of his practice. He sought not his own. His heart yearned with pity and brotherly affection for all the poor and suffering in the universe. Of him, the angel of Leigh Hunt's beautiful allegory might have written, in the golden book of remembrance, as he did of the good Abou ben Adhem, "*He loved his fellow-men.*"

ROBERT DINSMORE.

THE great charm of Scottish poetry consists in its simplicity and genuine, unaffected sympathy with the common joys and sorrows of daily life. It is a hometaught, household melody. It calls to mind the pastoral bleat on the hill-sides, the kirk-bells of a summer Sabbath, the song of the lark in the sunrise, the cry of the quail in the corn-land, the low of cattle, and the blithe carol of milkmaids "when the kye come hame" at gloaming. Meetings at fair and market, blushing betrothments, merry weddings, the joy of young maternity, the lights and shades of domestic life, its bereavements and partings, its chances and changes, its holy death-beds, and funerals solemnly beautiful in quiet kirk-yards—these furnish the hints of the immortal melodies of Burns, the sweet ballads of the Ettrick Shepherd and Allan Cunningham, and the rustic drama of Ramsay. It is the poetry of home, of nature, and the affections. All this is sadly wanting in our young literature. We have no songs; American domestic life has never been hallowed and beautified by the sweet and graceful and tender associations of poetry. We have no Yankee pastorals. Our rivers and streams turn mills and float rafts, and are otherwise as commendably useful as those of Scotland; but no quaint ballad, or simple song, reminds us that men and women have loved, met, and parted on their banks, or that beneath each roof within their valleys the tragedy and comedy of life has been enacted. Our poetry is cold and imitative; it seems more the product of overstrained intellects than the spontaneous outgushing of hearts warm with love, and strongly sympathizing with human nature as it actually exists about us, with the joys and griefs of the men and women whom we meet daily. Unhappily the opinion prevails that a poet must be also a philosopher, and hence it is, that much of our poetry is as indefinable in its mysticism as an Indian Brahman's commentary on his sacred books, or German metaphysics subjected to homœopathic dilution. It assumes to be prophetical, and its utterances are oracular. It tells of strange, vague emotions and yearnings, painfully suggestive of spiritual "groanings which cannot be uttered." If it "babbles o' green fields," and the common sights and sounds of nature, it is only for the purpose of finding some vague analogy between them and its internal experiences and longings. It leaves the warm and comfortable fireside of actual knowledge and human comprehension, and goes wailing and gibbering like a ghost about the impassable doors of mystery;

> It fain would be resolved
>   How things are done,
> And who the tailor is
>   That works for the man i' the sun.

How shall we account for this marked tendency in the literature of a shrewd, practical people? Is it that real life in New England lacks those conditions of poetry and romance which age, reverence, and superstition have gathered about it in the Old World? Is it that

> Ours are not Tempe's nor Arcadia's vales,

but are more famous for growing Indian corn and potatoes, and the manufacture of wooden ware and peddler notions, than for romantic associations and legendary interest? That our huge, unshapely shingle structures, blistering in the sun and glaring with windows, were evidently never reared by the spell of pastoral harmonies, as the walls of Thebes rose at the sound of the lyre of Amphion? That the habits of our people are too cool, cautious, undemonstrative to furnish the warp and woof of song and pastoral, and that their dialect and figures of speech, however richly significant and expressive in the autobiography of Sam Slick, or the satire of Hosea Bigelow and Ethan Spike, form a very awkward medium of sentiment and pathos? All this may be true. But the Yankee, after all, is a man, and as such, his history, could it be got at, must have more or less of poetic material in it; moreover, whether conscious of it or not, he also stands relieved against the background of Nature's beauty or sublimity. There is a poetical side to the commonplace of his incomings and outgoings; study him well, and you may frame an idyl of some sort from his apparently prosaic existence. Our poets, we must needs think, are deficient in that shiftiness, ready adaptation to circumstances, and ability of making the most of things, for which, as a people, we are proverbial. Can they make nothing of our Thanksgiving, that annual gathering of long-severed friends? Do they find nothing to their purpose in our apple-bees, huskings, berry-pickings, summer picnics, and winter sleigh-rides? Is there nothing available in our peculiarities of climate, scenery, customs, and political institutions? Does the Yankee leap into life, shrewd, hard, and speculating, armed, like Pallas, for a struggle with fortune? Are there not boys and girls, school loves and friendships, courtings and match-makings, hope and fear, and all the varied play of human passions—the keen struggles of gain, the mad grasping of ambition—sin and remorse, tearful repentance and holy aspirations? Who shall say that we have not all the essentials of the poetry of human life and simple nature, of the hearth and the farm-field? Here, then, is a mine unworked, a harvest ungathered. Who shall sink the shaft and thrust in the sickle?

And here let us say that the mere dilettante and the amateur ruralist may as well keep their hands off. The prize is not for them. He who would successfully strive for it, must be himself what he sings—part and parcel of the rural life of New England; one who has grown strong amid its healthful influences, familiar with all its details, and capable of detecting whatever of beauty, humor, or pathos, pertain to it; one who has added to his book-lore the large experience of an active participation in the rugged toil, the hearty amusements, the trials, and the pleasures he describes.

We have been led to these reflections by an incident which has called up before us the homespun figure of an old friend of our boyhood, who had the good sense to discover that the poetic element existed in the simple home life of a country farmer, although himself unable to give a very creditable expression of it. He had the "vision" indeed, but the "faculty divine" was wanting, or, if he possessed it in any degree, as Thersites says of the wit of Ajax, "It would not out, but lay coldly in him like fire in the flint."

While engaged this morning in looking over a large exchange list of newspapers, a few stanzas of poetry in the Scottish dialect attracted our attention. As we read them, like a wizard's rhyme they seemed to have the power of bearing us back to the past. They had long ago graced the columns of that solitary sheet which once a week diffused happiness over our fireside circle, making us acquainted, in our lonely nook, with the goings-on of the great world. The verses, we are now constrained to admit, are not remarkable in themselves—truth, and simple nature only; yet how our young hearts responded to them! Twenty years ago there were fewer verse-makers than at present; and as our whole stock of light literature consisted of Ellwood's Davideis, and the selections of Lindley Murray's

English Reader, it is not improbable that we were in a condition to overestimate the contributions to the poet's corner of our village newspaper. Be that as it may, we welcome them as we would the face of an old friend, for they somehow remind us of the scent of hay-mows, the breath of cattle, the fresh greenery by the brook-side, the moist earth broken by the coulter and turned up to the sun and winds of May. This particular piece, which follows, is entitled "The Sparrow," and was occasioned by the crushing of a bird's nest by the author, while plowing among his corn. It has something of the simple tenderness of Burns.

Poor innocent and hapless sparrow!
Why should my mold-board gie thee sorrow!
This day thou'lt chirp and mourn the morrow
 Wi' anxious breast;
The plow has turned the mold'ring furrow
 Deep o'er thy nest!

Just i' the middle o' the hill
Thy nest was placed wi' curious skill;
There I espied thy little bill
 Beneath the shape.
In that sweet bower, secure frae ill,
 Thine eggs were laid.

Five corns o' maize had there been drappit,
An' through the stalks thy head was pappit,
The drawing nowt couldna be stappit
 I quickly foun';
Syne frae thy cozie nest thou happit,
 Wild fluttering roun'.

The sklentin stane beguiled the sheer,
In vain I tried the plow to steer,
A wee bit stumpie i' the rear
    Cam' 'tween my legs,
An' to the jee-side gart me veer
    An' crush thine eggs.

Alas! alas! my bonnie birdie!
Thy faithful mate flits round to guard thee.
Connubial love!—a pattern worthy
    The pious priest!
What savage heart could be sae hardy
    As wound thy breast?

Ah me! it was nae fau't o' mine;
It gars me greet to see thee pine.
It may be serves His great design
    Who governs all;
Omniscience tents wi' eyes divine
    The sparrow's fall!

How much like thine are human dools,
Their sweet wee bairns laid i' the mools?
The Sovereign Power who nature rules,
    Hath said so be it;
But poor blin' mortals are sic fools
    They canna see it.

Nae doubt that He who first did mate us,
Has fixed our lot as sure as fate is,
An' when he wounds He disna hate us,
    But anely this,
He'll gar the ills which here await us
    Yield lastin' bliss.

In the early part of the eighteenth century, a considerable number of Presbyterians of Scotch descent, from the north of Ireland, emigrated to the New World. In the spring of 1719 the inhabitants of Haverhill, on the Merrimac, saw them passing up the river in several canoes, one of which unfortunately upset in the rapids above the village. The following fragment of a ballad celebrating this event, has been handed down to the present time, and may serve to show the feelings, even then, of the old English settlers toward the Irish emigrants:

They began to scream and bawl,
  As out they tumbled one and all,
And, if the Devil had spread his net,
  He could have made a glorious haul!

The new-comers proceeded up the river, and, landing opposite to the Uncanoonuc Hills, on the present site of Manchester, proceeded inland to Beaver Pond. Charmed with the appearance of the country, they resolved here to terminate their wanderings. Under a venerable oak on the margin of the little lake, they knelt down with their minister, Jamie McGregore, and laid, in prayer and thanksgiving, the foundation of their settlement. In a few years they had cleared large fields, built substantial stone and frame dwellings, and a large and commodious meeting-house; wealth had accumulated around them, and they had everywhere the reputation of a shrewd and thriving community. They were the first in New England to cultivate the potato, which their neighbors for a long time regarded as a pernicious root, altogether unfit for a Christian stomach. Every lover of that invaluable esculent has reason to remember with gratitude the settlers of Londonderry.

Their moral acclimation in Ireland had not been without its effect upon their character. Side by side with a Presbyterianism as austere as that of John Knox, had grown up something of the wild Milesian humor, love of convivial excitement and merry-making. Their long prayers and fierce zeal in behalf of orthodox tenets, only served, in the eyes of their Puritan neighbors, to make more glaring still the scandal of their marked social irregularities. It became a common saying in the region roundabout, that, "the Derry Presbyterians would never give up a *pint* of doctrine, or a *pint* of rum." Their second minister was an old scarred fighter, who had signalized himself in the stout defense of Londonderry, when James II and his Papists were thundering at its gates. Agreeably to his death-bed directions, his old fellow-soldiers, in their leathern doublets and battered steel caps, bore him to his grave, firing over him the same rusty muskets which had swept down rank after rank of the men of Amalek at the Derry siege.

Ere long the celebrated Derry Fair was established in imitation of those with which they had been familiar in Ireland. Thither annually came all manner of horse-jockeys and peddlers, gentlemen and beggars, fortune-tellers, wrestlers, dancers and fiddlers, gay young farmers and buxom maidens. Strong drink abounded. They who had good-naturedly wrestled and joked together in the morning not unfrequently closed the day with a fight, until, like the revelers of Donnybrook,

> Their hearts were soft with whisky,
> And their heads were soft with blows.

A wild, frolicking, drinking, fiddling, courting, horse-racing, riotous merry-making—a sort of Protestant carnival—relaxing the grimness of Puritanism for leagues around it.

In the midst of such a community, and partaking of all its influences, Robert Dinsmore, the author of the poem I have quoted, was born about the middle of the last century. His paternal ancestor, John, younger son of a Laird of Achenmead, who left the banks of the Tweed for the green fertility of Northern Ireland, had emigrated to New England some forty years before, and, after a rough experience of Indian captivity in the wild woods of Maine, had settled down among his old neighbors in Londonderry. Until nine years of age, Robert never saw a school. He was a short time under the tuition of an old British soldier, who had strayed into the settlement after the French war, "at which time," he says in a letter to a friend, "I learned to repeat the shorter and larger catechisms. These, with the Scripture proofs annexed to them, confirmed me in the orthodoxy of my forefathers, and I hope I shall ever remain an evidence of the truth of what the wise man said, 'Train up a child in the way he should go, and when he is old he will not depart from it.'" He afterward took lessons with one Master McKeen, who used to spend much of his time in hunting squirrels with his pupils. He learned to read and write; and the old man always insisted that he should have done well at ciphering also, had he not fallen in love with Molly Park. At the age of eighteen he enlisted in the revolutionary army, and was at the battle of Saratoga. On his return he married his fair Molly, settled down as a farmer in Windham, formerly a part of Londonderry, and before he was thirty years of age became an elder in the church, of the creed and observances of which he was always a zealous and resolute defender. From occasional passages in his poems, it is evident that the instructions which he derived from the pulpit were not unlike those which Burns suggested as needful for the unlucky lad whom he was commending to his friend Hamilton:

> Ye'll catechise him ilka quirk,
> An' shore him weel wi' hell.

In a humorous poem, entitled "Spring's Lament," he thus describes the consternation produced in the meeting-house at sermon time by a dog, who, in search of his mistress, rattled and scraped at the "west porch door":

> The vera priest was scared himsel',
> His sermon he could hardly spell,
> Auld carlins fancied they could smell
>   The brimstone matches;
> They thought he was some imp o' hell,
>   In quest o' wretches.

He lived to a good old age, a home-loving, unpretending farmer, cultivating his acres with his own horny hands, and cheering the long rainy days and winter evenings with homely rhyme. Most of his pieces were written in the dialect of his ancestors, which was well understood by his neighbors and friends, the only audience upon which he could venture to calculate. He loved all old things, old language, old customs, old theology. In a rhyming letter to his cousin Silas, he says:

Though Death our ancestors has cleekit,
An' under clods them closely steekit,
We'll mark the place their chimneys reekit;
Their native tongue we yet wad speak it,
Wi' accent glib.

He wrote sometimes to amuse his neighbors, often to soothe their sorrow under domestic calamity, or to give expression to his own. With little of that delicacy of taste which results from the attrition of fastidious and refined society, and altogether too truthful and matter-of-fact to call in the aid of imagination, he describes in the simplest and most direct terms the circumstances in which he found himself, and the impressions which these circumstances had made on his own mind. He calls things by their right names; no euphemism, or transcendentalism—the plainer and commoner the better. He tells us of his farm life, its joys and sorrows, its mirth and care, with no embellishment, with no concealment of repulsive and ungraceful features. Never having seen a nightingale, he makes no attempt to describe the fowl; but he has seen the night-hawk, at sunset, cutting the air above him, and he tells of it. Side by side with his waving corn-fields and orchard-blooms, we have the barn-yard and pig-sty. Nothing which was necessary to the comfort and happiness of his home and avocation was to him "common or unclean." Take, for instance, the following, from a poem written at the close of autumn, after the death of his wife:

> No more may I the Spring Brook trace,
> No more with sorrow view the place
> *Where Mary's wash-tub stood;*
> No more may wander there alone,
> *And lean upon the mossy stone,*
> *Where once she piled her wood.*
> *'Twas there she bleached her linen cloth,*
> By yonder bass-wood tree;
> From that sweet stream she made her broth,
> Her pudding and her tea.
> That stream, whose waters running,
> O'er mossy root and stone,
> Made ringing and singing
> *Her voice could match alone.*

We envy not the man who can sneer at this simple picture. It is honest as nature herself. An old and lonely man looks back upon the young years of his wedded life. Can we not look with him? The sunlight of a summer morning is weaving itself with the leafy shadows of the bass-tree, beneath which a fair and ruddy-cheeked young woman, with her full, rounded arms bared to the elbow, bends not ungracefully to her task, pausing ever and anon to play with the bright-eyed child beside her, and mingling her songs with the pleasant murmurings of gliding water! Alas! as the old man looks, he hears that voice, which perpetually sounds to us all from the past—NO MORE!

Let us look at him in his more genial mood. Take the opening lines of his "Thanksgiving Day." What a plain, hearty picture of substantial comfort!

When corn is in the garret stored,
And sauce in cellar well secured,
When good fat beef we can afford,
    And things that 're dainty,
With good sweet cider on our board,
    And pudding plenty;

When stock, well housed, may chew the cud,
And at my door a pile of wood,
A rousing fire to warm my blood,
    Blest sight to see!
It puts my rustic muse in mood
    To sing for thee.

If he needs a simile, he takes the nearest at hand. In a letter to his daughter he says:

That mine is not a longer letter,
The cause is not the want of matter—
Of that there's plenty, worse or better;
    But *like a mill,*
Whose stream beats back with surplus water,
    The wheel stands still.

Something of the humor of Burns gleams out occasionally from the sober decorum of his verses. In an epistle to his friend Betton, high sheriff of the county, who had sent to him for a peck of seed corn, he says:

> Soon plantin' time will come again;
> Syne may the heavens gie us rain,
> An' shining heat to bless ilk plain
>   An' fertile hill,
> An' gar the loads o' yellow grain,
>   Our garrets fill.
>
> As long as I hae food and clothing,
> An' still am hale and fier and breathing,
> Ye's get the corn——and may be ae thing
>   Ye'll do for me
> (Though God forbid)—hang me for naething
>   An' lose your fee.

And on receiving a copy of some verses written by a lady, he talks in a sad way for a Presbyterian deacon:

> Were she some Aborigine squaw,
> Wha sings so sweet by nature's law,
> I'd meet her in a hazle shaw,
>   Or some green loany,
> And make her, tawny phiz and 'a,
>   My welcome crony.

The practical philosophy of the stout, jovial rhymer was but little affected by the sour-featured asceticism of the elder. He says:

We'll eat and drink, and cheerful take
Our portions for the Donor's sake,
For thus the Word of Wisdom spake—
    Man can't do better;
Nor can we by our labors make
    The Lord our debtor.

A quaintly characteristic correspondence in rhyme between the Deacon and Parson McGregore, evidently "birds o' ane feather," is still in existence. The minister, in acknowledging the epistle of his old friend, commences his reply as follows:

Did e'er a cuif tak' up a quill,
Wha ne'er did aught that he did well,
To gar the muses rant an' reel,
    An' flaunt and swagger,
Nae doubt ye'll say 'tis that daft chiel
    Old Dite McGregore!

The reply is in the same strain, and may serve to give the reader some idea of the old gentleman as a religious controversialist:

My reverend friend an' kind McGregore,
Although thou ne'er was ca'd a bragger,
Thy muse, I'm sure nane e'er was glegger—
    Thy Scottish lays
Might gar Socinians fa' or stagger,
    E'en in their ways.

When Unitarian champions dare thee,
Goliah-like, an' think to scare thee,
Dear Davie, fear not, they'll ne'er waur thee;
    But draw thy sling,
Weel loaded frae the gospel quarry,
    An' gie 't a fling.

The last time I saw him he was chaffering in the market-place of my native village, swapping potatoes and onions and pumpkins for tea, coffee, molasses, and, if the truth be told, New England rum. Three-score years and ten, to use his own words,

> Hung o'er his back,
> And bent him like a muckle pack,

yet he still stood stoutly and sturdily in his thick shoes of cowhide, like one accustomed to tread independently the soil of his own acres—his broad, honest face, seamed by care and darkened by exposure to "all the airts that blow," and his white hair flowing in patriarchal glory beneath his felt hat. A genial, jovial, large-hearted old man, simple as a child, and betraying neither in look nor manner that he was accustomed to

> Feed on thoughts which voluntary move
> Harmonious numbers.

Peace to him! A score of modern dandies and sentimentalists could ill supply the place of this one honest man. In the ancient burial-ground of Windham, by the side of his "beloved Molly," and in view of the old meeting-house, there is a mound of earth, where, every spring, green grasses tremble in the wind and the warm sunshine calls out the flowers. There, gathered like one of his own ripe sheaves, the farmer-poet sleeps with his fathers.

www.ingramcontent.com/pod-product-compliance
Lightning Source LLC
LaVergne TN
LVHW010235110826
845151LV00004B/1298

* 9 7 8 1 4 2 5 5 2 4 9 6 8 *